The Other Mexico

a guide to ancient wonders
and modern pleasures in Mexico

by

E. J. Guarino

Golden West Publishers

Cover design by Bruce Robert Fischer/The Art Studio

Maps and site plans by Thayer Durell, Jr.

Photographs by the author

Library of Congress Cataloging-in-Publication Data

Guarino, E. J.
The other Mexico.

Includes index.
1. Indians of Mexico--Antiquities--Guide-books.
2. Mexico--Antiquities--Guide-books. 3. Mexico--
Description and travel--1981- --Guide-books.
I. Title.
F1219.G92 1988 917.2'04834 88-6105
ISBN 0-914846-36-1

Printed in the United States of America

Golden West Publishers
4113 N. Longview Ave.
Phoenix, AZ 85014, USA

Dedication

To Thayer Durell, Jr., and
to Kathleen Guarino-Burns
whose helpfulness and patience
made this book possible,
and to my parents
without whose sacrifices
nothing would have been possible.

My special thanks to Rosemary Martino
and Carol Buckley
for their help and encouragement.

CONTENTS

MAPS

PREFACE

Like so many other travelers, for years I avoided Mexico like the plague, totally unaware of the fantastic experiences I was missing. Thinking back to those days always brings an ironic smile to my face because ever since my first visit I have come to love Mexico as I never thought I would. My first trip to Mexico wasn't well planned but I must have done something right because afterwards I became obsessed with the country. I just couldn't get enough.

In those days, all I knew of Mexico's ancient past were a few facts about the Maya and the Aztecs. I was totally unaware of any other groups that peopled ancient Mexico. My first visit to the National Museum of Anthropology was to change all that. It hit me like a right hook. Up until that point I had thought I was rather well educated. How could I have missed all this? I searched my memory. I didn't remember hearing about these things in my history classes. Like a glutton I dashed from room to room devouring all that I could. I now proceed through the museum at a slower pace savoring all the beauty it contains but I still feel as though I'm in a wonderland for grown-ups.

It was also at the time of this first trip that major excavations had begun in Mexico City on Templo Mayor, the Aztecs major temple, which had been buried for centuries. The site was not yet open to the public but there was a convention of sociologists in the city and they were allowed in. Every morning buses, with the word SOCIOLOGISTS emblazoned on the front, pulled up in front of my hotel.

Desperately I tried to figure out a way of passing myself off as one of them. Since none of my ideas seemed good, much less normal, I gave up and had to content myself with peering at the remains of the great temple through a hole in a fence. It was not until a few years later that I realized my goal and entered the site with the rest of the public like a good little sheep.

Mexico City has continued to be a constant revelation to me. Each visit produces things I never knew about before. I had never heard of Diego Rivera, for example, so I came to his work an innocent. His murals in the National Palace were unlike anything I had ever seen before. Their images seem to scream out, "Here is Mexico in all her glory and torment."

For me, some of the capital's most fondly remembered pleasures have nothing to do with anything as high-minded as history or art. My idea of heaven is eating an early morning breakfast, overlooking the Zocalo, on the tiny "terrace" of the Gran Hotel de la Ciudad de Mexico. With the Cathedral and the National Palace as a backdrop, one has a front row seat as the great plaza awakens and comes to colorful life.

If I really want to spoil myself I have lunch at the rooftop restaurant of the Hotel Majestic. It, too, overlooks the plaza and is so romantic a spot that I have, while merely on a stop over in the capital, dashed there by cab from the airport just to have a meal.

Of course, the country's primary draw for me is not its restaurants. I have found Mexico's archaeological sites far more interesting and safer to visit than those of Europe or the Middle East.

Not far from Mexico City is Teotihuacan. It was the first of Mexico's ancient cities I was to visit. I couldn't believe that mere humans had created this place. Surely, I thought, some gods or space visitors, at the very least, did this. As I ever so nervously climbed the largest of the pyramids, Mexican women in spiked heels zipped by me.

My next experience with archaeology was almost my last. The first thing one sees at the ruins of Uxmal, in the Yucatan, is the Pyramid of the Magician. Seeing it I knew I had to climb it. What could be easier, I thought. After all, wasn't I an experienced pyramid climber by now? Up I went, holding on to the chain that is there as an aid. With each step higher, I began to realize that this was not one of my better ideas. By the time I reached the top I knew it had been a downright stupid idea.

At the summit, I immediately did what any other hearty traveler would have done. I panicked. When I finally realized that it would not be feasible to spend the rest of my life atop a pyramid, despite the spectacular view, I came up with a plan. Sitting on my rear end and clinging for dear life to the chain, which by now had become a life line, I made the slow descent. Just as I felt that things were going rather smoothly, I noticed that as I was descending the pyramid a little old woman was ascending. I realized that we would soon meet and that one of us would have to let go of the precious chain and go around the other. Since you are reading these words, I'm sure that you can figure out which one of us didn't let go.

Fortunately, all of my other archaeological encounters were not so melodramatic. I'll never forget my surprise when I drove up to the small pyramid of Tenayuca and a woman opened the door to her house and out poured a herd of sheep. Here, too, I met a group of Mexican school children happily romping up and down the pyramid's steep steps. They waved excitedly but shyly and indicated that they would like their picture taken. When I obliged I was met with warm hand shakes and greetings of Buenos Dias and Mucho Gusto.

Then, too, there was the caretaker at the Aztec pyramid of Santa Cecilia Acatitlan who had the kindness to let me enter an hour before opening time because I had come from so far away. What a pleasure to have the pyramid, the museum and the gardens all to myself! It was, indeed, a special moment.

The day I decided to visit the small village of Teotitlan del Valle, near Oaxaca, with the hope of buying a beautiful rug made by the Zapotec Indians is a special memory for quite a different reason. At one stop, as my driver and the rugmaker were opening numerous rugs for my inspection out rolled a scorpion. Seeing its small claws, I, at first, could not figure out how a baby lobster had gotten so far inland.

In a split second I realized what it was and backed away as if I were facing a cobra. The Mexican reaction was in marked contrast to mine. My driver said, "Ah, un animalito," picked up the scorpion by the tail and unceremoniously tossed it out the door.

Mexico has filled my heart with countless unique memories: discovering, for myself, the treasures of Oaxaca's museums, descending to Pacal's tomb at Palenque, finally seeing the Pyramid of the Niches at El Tajin, and having to take shelter in the Temple of the Jaguar during a rainstorm at Chichen Itza. It is the knowledge that each trip to Mexico will provide me with special remembrances that keeps me returning to that fascinating land.

INTRODUCTION
Where the Smart Set Goes

Beyond its beaches, and even beyond its justly famous colonial cities, there lies another, ancient Mexico. Though distant in time, it is geographically near and surprisingly accessible. However, most travelers are unaware of Mexico's ancient cities and have overlooked them for years.

Before any European ever stepped foot in the New World, civilizations flourished in Mexico. To the Europeans who ventured to this new land, the native peoples they encountered were heathen savages and inferior. This prejudice of cultural superiority has persisted down to the present and has influenced our historical point of view.

Although Mexico contains a vast wealth of architectural wonders, relatively few people are aware of them. Who has not heard of the Pyramids of Egypt, the Acropolis of Athens or the Coliseum of Rome? Yet, how many have heard of Uxmal, Monte Alban or El Tajin? Most school children have heard of Tutankhamun of Egypt while few, if any, know of Lord Pacal of Palenque whose tomb lay undisturbed within a pyramid until only a few decades ago! Fortunately, this is beginning to change.

Many people still avoid traveling to Mexico because of deep-seated, but misinformed, beliefs. Of course, the strongest convictions are those held concerning Mexico's drinking water. This is the area of greatest concern for most travelers. It seems that most people believe a visit to Mexico is a guarantee of becoming ill. This simply is not true.

Any change in water, diet, altitude, routine or time zone can, and often does, produce stomach upsets. This can be true of any destination, yet people seem to associate this problem solely with Mexico. However, by oberving a few simple measures, problems of this nature can be kept to a minimum, if not avoided completely. The unnecessary fear of illness should not deter a traveler from beholding Mexico's ancient wonders.

Sadly, however, even among those travelers who do visit Mexico, relatively few venture beyond Mexico City or the beach resorts. For some the capital is Mexico. This is no more true of Mexico than it is of the United States or any other country. For still others, Mexico holds no interest beyond a few major beach resorts. Perhaps these attitudes can simply be attributed to a lack of awareness. The belief exists among many travelers that Mexico's archaeological sites are difficult to visit.

On the contrary, most major sites can easily be visited by rental car, bus, cab or guided tour. Because of the locations of Mexico's archaeological treasures, it is quite feasible to combine visits to these sites with stays at comfortable and charming hotels in resorts and colonial cities. It is also possible to stay at hotels at some of the sites themselves. This provides nourishment and rest for both mind and body.

Mexico's cultural heritage is rich and varied. The Mexican people are justly proud of this heritage and most will go out of their way to show a visitor aspects of the country that might otherwise be easily missed. Knowledge of Spanish is helpful but not essential. Mexicans are genuinely delighted by any interest in their culture or their language. Any effort to see beyond the familiar misconceptions and stereotypes will result in a much more satisfying travel experience.

Chapter 1

MEXICO CITY

Capital Ideas

Mexico City is the gateway to the rest of the country and is the best introduction to the many cultures that are Mexico. A visit to the capital is essential for those who may not be familiar with Mexico's ancient civilizations. Of the many cultural attractions the city has to offer, the Museum of Anthropology, the Museum of the City of Mexico, Templo Mayor and the Templo Mayor Museum should not be missed.

A Nation's Pride

The National Museum of Anthropology in Chapultepec Park is easily reached from any part of the capital. Travel within Mexico City is easy and inexpensive by taxi but the National Museum of Anthropology can also be reached by taking a No. 100 bus, marked "Auditorio," which runs along Reforma. By subway, the museum can be reached by getting off at the Chapultepec station and then walking through the park along Reforma. From Tuesday through Saturday the museum is open from 9 a.m. until 7 p.m. On Sunday it is open from 10 a.m. until 6 p.m.

This museum offers the visitor an overview of life in pre-Columbian Mexico. Pre-Columbian does not simply refer to those cultures which existed before the entry of Columbus into the New World. It also refers to cultures, like that of the Aztecs, which flourished well after his arrival. Exhibited throughout this museum are artifacts from numerous sites throughout Mexico. Through masterpieces of artistic expression, the visitor is introduced to the cultures of the Olmecs, Mayas, Zapotecs and Aztecs, among others.

The Layout of the Museum

Contents of the Museum are presented on two floors. The first floor is devoted to the pre-Hispanic cultures, while the second floor presents the modern cultures of Mexico. Visiting both sections is highly recommended for a better understanding of Mexico's diverse cultural heritage, since the pre-Columbian peoples were the ancestors of Mexico's modern indigenous population.

The pre-Hispanic section presents a vast array of artifacts which

MEXICO CITY

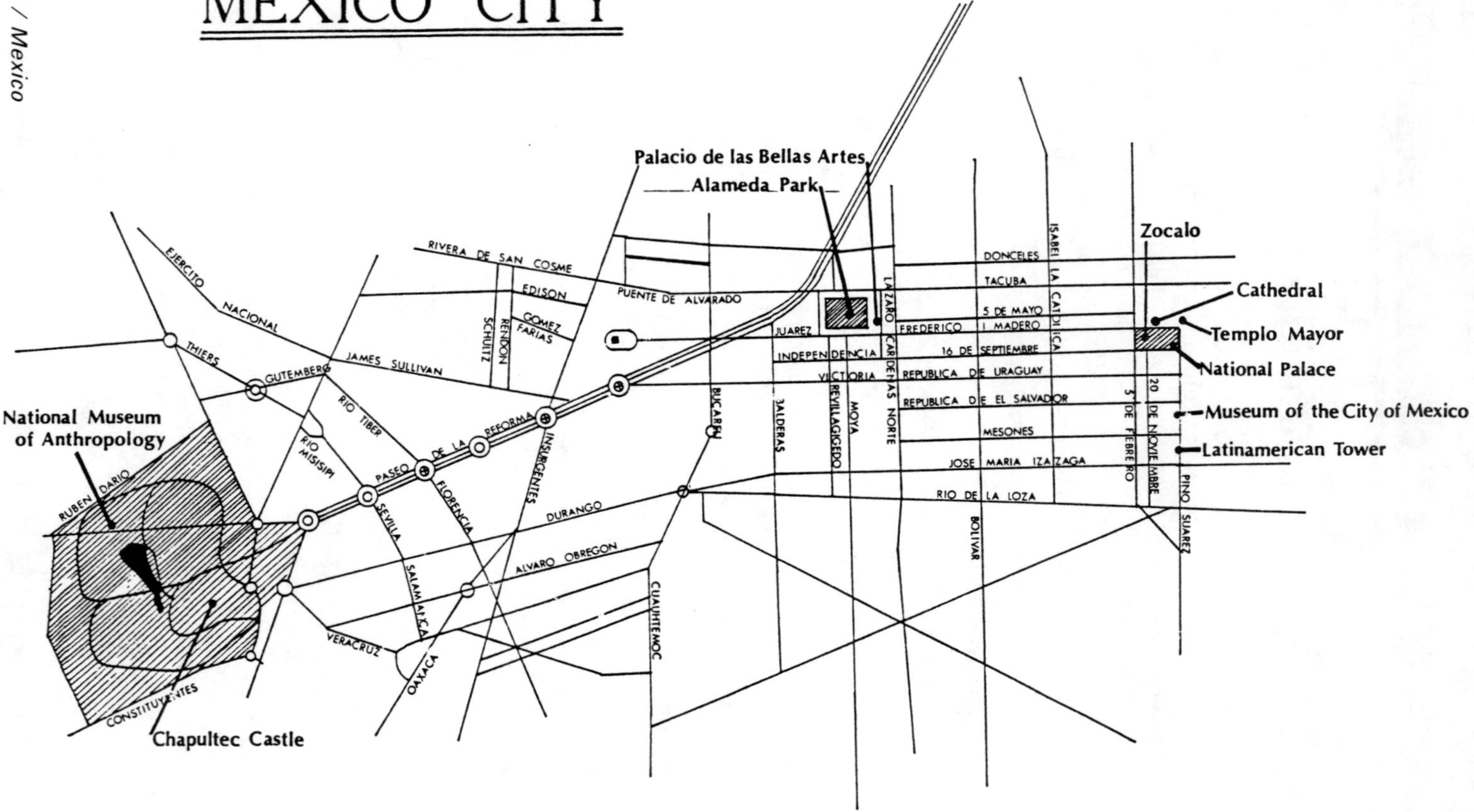

Palacio de las Bellas Artes
Alameda Park
Zocalo
Cathedral
Templo Mayor
National Palace
Museum of the City of Mexico
Latinamerican Tower
National Museum of Anthropology
Chapultec Castle
DONCELES
TACUBA
5 DE MAYO
FREDERICO I MADERO
16 DE SEPTIEMBRE
REPUBLICA DE URAGUAY
REPUBLICA DE EL SALVADOR
MESONES
JOSE MARIA IZAZAGA
RIO DE LA LOZA
ISABEL LA CATOLICA
5 DE FEBRERO
20 DE NOVIEMBRE
PINO SUAREZ
BOLIVAR
LAZARO CARDENAS NORTE
MOYA
REVILLAGIGEDO
BALDERAS
JUAREZ
INDEPENDENCIA
VICTORIA
BUCARELI
CUAUHTEMOC
PUENTE DE ALVARADO
RIVERA DE SAN COSME
EDISON
GOMEZ FARIAS
RENDON
SCHULTZ
JAMES SULLIVAN
EJERCITO NACIONAL
THIERS
GUTEMBERG
RIO TIBER
RIO MISISIPI
PASEO DE LA REFORMA
INSURGENTES
FLORENCIA
SEVILLA
SALAMANCA
DURANGO
ALVARO OBREGON
VERACRUZ
OAXACA
RUBEN DARIO
CONSTITUYENTES

range from tiny, intricately carved pieces to monumental stone carvings. Most of the collection is displayed indoors, but a few of the larger works, such as a 200 ton carving possibly representing the rain god Tlaloc and a monumental, stone Olmec head, are presented in an outdoor setting. A walk through the museum acquaints the visitor with the depth and variety of pre-Columbian achievement. One can see examples in a wide range of sizes and artistic mediums. Artists' skills are well represented in jade, gold, stucco, stone and countless ceramic pieces.

Among the most striking exhibits are the Aztec Calendar Stone, a reproduction of a portion of the Temple of Quetzalcoatl at Teotihuacan, a copy of the frescoes at Bonampak, and a reproduction of the tomb and sarcophagus of Lord Pacal of Palenque.

Photographers Take Note

Once again, photography is permitted at the National Museum of Anthropology. However, in order to photograph, it is necessary to get a permit at the museum for a fee of approximately two dollars U.S. Permits can be obtained at a counter behind and to the left of the book store.

Since flash is not permitted, it is best to photograph in the museum with high speed film. It is a good idea to bring such film with you since it can be difficult to obtain in Mexico. Some of the airport shops may carry high speed film, but don't count on it.

Those shooting 35mm color transparencies will probably get the best results by using 400 ASA film BUT SHOOTING IT AT 800 ASA. When having the film developed, be sure to indicate it was "boosted" to 800 ASA. The film MUST be put in a special envelope to insure correct processing at the lab.

For prints, 1000 ASA will work under most lighting conditions in the museum. In some instances, 200 ASA and 400 ASA may also give good results.

Aztec Human Sacrifice

The Aztecs often created on a grand scale. The Calendar Stone is an excellent example of this inclination. The stone was unearthed during an excavation in the Zocalo, the main square of the city. The stone was originally painted in bright colors which now are not easily discernible. In the center of the stone the sun is represented with a protruding tongue and a human heart in each hand. Among other things, the stone represents the Aztec belief in the fifth sun which needed to be sustained by human sacrifice.

It was believed that there had been four suns before the present one. Each of these suns and its world had been destroyed. According to myth, after the fourth world had been destroyed by flood, the fifth sun came into being when a god immolated himself. Other gods also sacrificed themselves in order to give the new sun life and motion.

The Aztecs felt they were charged with nourishing the present sun and the other gods with similar sacrifices and offered human blood and hearts. Furthermore, to the Aztecs the ritual of blood sacrifice may have been an act of reciprocity since they believed that humans were created by the god Quetzalcoatl through the spilling of his own blood. This was one of the practices which the Europeans found abhorrent. To the Aztecs it was an essential part of their worship.

A Misconception Vanishes

Reproduced in another hall is a section of the Temple of Quetzalcoatl as it originally looked. Unlike the actual temple at Teotihuacan, it is awash with color. The numerous serpent heads, each surrounded by a feather collar, can clearly be seen. An exhibit such as this removes the misconception that pre-Hispanic architecture was stark and colorless. On the contrary, the buildings were brightly painted and anything but drab. For those planning to visit Teotihuacan, this exhibit, as well as the artifacts from this site, add a dimension of understanding which might otherwise be missing.

Places Rarely Seen

Through its exhibits the museum also affords visitors the opportunity of seeing aspects of archaeological sites which are not easily reached by the average traveler. The frescoes of Bonampak are a case in point. Because Bonampak lies deep in the jungles of Chiapas, and because it takes some effort to reach, it is not a heavily visited site. According to recent reports, in an attempt to prevent further deterioration of the wall paintings, visitors may no longer be allowed access to the Temple of the Frescoes. The frescoes of Bonampak are masterpieces of color, design and execution. Before the discovery of these murals it was not known that the Maya worked in this medium. Furthermore, the content of the frescoes brought to light much new information about these people and contradicted the notion that they were peace-loving. These wall paintings bring the Maya and their culture vividly to life. The reproductions allow travelers to see the beauty of the frescoes with clarity and ease.

Deep Inside a Hidden Tomb

Whether or not one is planning to visit Palenque, the replica of Pacal's tomb should be seen. Except for the sarcophagus lid, all of the pieces found in the tomb were removed from Palenque and are displayed in the National Museum of Anthropology.

This exhibit gives the visitor a sense of what it must have been like when, after lying undisturbed for centuries, the lid of the sarcophagus was raised, revealing Pacal. This is an enlightening prelude to a visit to Palenque where one can descend to the real tomb.

Masterpieces and Aids to Understanding

Throughout the museum there are countless masterpieces of pre-Hispanic art, as well as numerous photographs and models, which all serve to make the visitor aware of ancient Mexico's numerous cultures. The museum's exhibits also shed light on the customs and achievements of these cultures.

Among the many masterpieces, the museum houses one of the monumental, stone Atlantes from Tula, a monolithic statue of the Aztec goddess Coatlicue, a large bas-relief from the Temple of the Cross at Palenque, an Aztec ceremonial vase in the form of a huge jaguar and the huge and magnificently carved Stone of Tizoc found at Templo Mayor.

At various points within the museum, there are greatly enlarged photographs of many of Mexico's archaeological sites. These photographs help the visitor to see the museum's many artifacts in their proper context. The photographs also serve to make one aware of the visual beauty of the sites and, hopefully, more people will become interested enough to visit some of these areas.

Also very helpful are the excellent models and full-scale reproductions found in the museum. Among these are scale models of such sites as Yaxchilan, Tenochtitlan, Cholula and Tulum. There are also models of some of the more famous structures at a number of major archaeological sites. Represented

NATIONAL MUSEUM OF ANTHROPOLOGY - MEXICO CITY

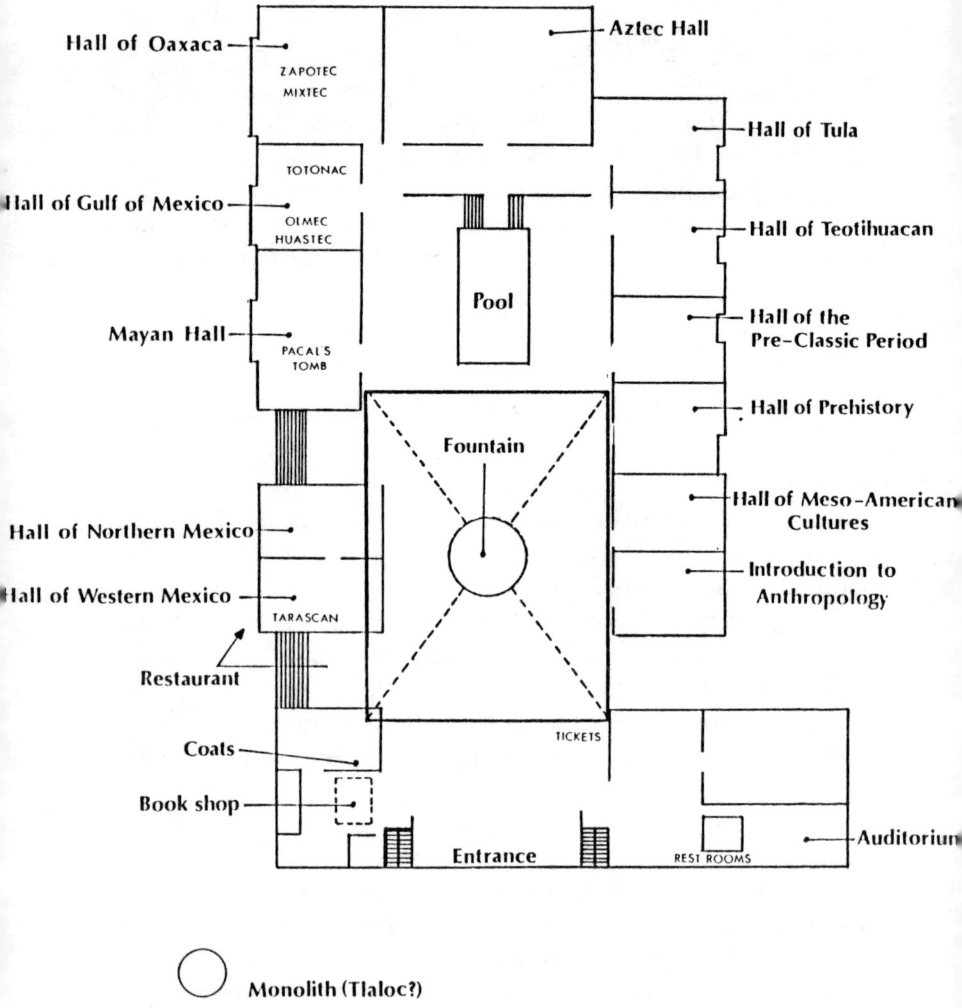

are El Castillo at Chichen Itza, the Pyramid of the Niches at El Tajin, and the pyramid at Tenayuca, as well as models of the market and ball court of Tenochtitlan. Besides the full-scale reproduction of Pacal's tomb at Palenque, there are also exact replicas of Tomb 7 and Tomb 104 at Monte Alban. These reproductions show what the interiors of the tombs looked like at the time of their discovery. The museum also displays an excellent panoramic painting which shows the entire Aztec capital of Tenochtitlan. The painting clearly illustrates the location of the city in the center of a lake and shows the causeways which connected the capital to the mainland.

The National Museum of Anthropology houses the greatest collection of Mexican pre-Columbian treasures in the world. As such, it displays a vast array of the national patrimony and is a source of great pride to the Mexican people.

A Gem Unknown To Most Tourists

Although small in comparison to the National Museum of Anthropology and unknown to most tourists, the Museum of the City of Mexico is a small gem containing a wealth of interesting and informative exhibits. The museum is devoted solely to development in the Valley of Mexico and is an excellent introduction to both Templo Mayor and the Aztecs who built it. The museum is located three blocks south of the Zocalo on Pino Suarez. The museum is open Tuesday through Sunday from 9:30 a.m. until 7:30 p.m.

One of the most interesting aspects of the Museum is the model of Tenochtitlan, the Aztec capital, which lies under the modern capital. One can clearly see the general layout of the ceremonial center of the ancient capital as well as the location of Templo Mayor in relation to the rest of the city.

The City Founded by an Eagle

Tenochtitlan was an island city situated in the middle of Lake Texcoco and connected to the mainland by causeways. Before the founding of Tenochtitlan, the Aztecs had been a wandering tribe settling in one place for a few years and then, at the command of their god, Huitzilopochtli, moving on. They had been told to settle where they came upon an eagle perched on a cactus and eating a serpent. (Some legends say a bird.)

Just such a sign was seen on the island in Lake Texcoco and the Aztecs set about building their city. At its center they constructed a great temple and at the top they built a sanctuary to Huitzilopochtli, their war god, and another to Tlaloc, god of rain and fertility. At the height of its power Tenochtitlan was home to some 300,000 people. This ancient metropolis was built without the aid of the wheel or beasts of burden.

After the destruction of the Aztec capital, the Spanish proceeded to build a new city upon its ruins and the remains of the ancient capital were entombed beneath the modern one. From Aztec times the area of the city was expanded through the use of landfill. The practice was continued and what was once an island capital became one that was landlocked.

Sacred Heart of an Ancient City

As the Cathedral is to the modern city, Templo Mayor was the sacred heart of the Aztec capital. It was the geographical and spiritual center of life in Tenochtitlan. The current excavation at Templo Mayor is one of the most recent and exciting archaeological finds in the Americas. Walking about Templo Mayor the visitor can sense the excitement of discovery. The ruins and the new museum are open to the public Tuesday to Sunday, 9 a.m. to 5 p.m.

Dismembered Goddess

Since the late 1700s, various excavations had been undertaken in the area of the Zocalo, but it was not until 1978 that the great Temple of the Aztecs was found. The first discovery was a colossal stone relief of the goddess Coyolxauhqui, sister of Huitzilopochtli. This circular stone represents the defeat of Coyolxauhqui at the hands of her brother. Coyolxauhqui was the moon goddess and Huitzilopochtli was associated with the sun. They fought for dominance of the heavens. According to Aztec myth, there was an enmity between the divine siblings even while Huitzilopochtli was in his mother's womb. His sister was enraged over the manner of Huitzilopochtli's conception which occurred when their mother Coatlicue tucked a ball of feathers she had found under her garments. Feeling threatened by the new child and shamed because the father was unknown, Coyolxauhqui and her other siblings, the stars, declared they would kill their mother. Though still unborn, Huitzilopochtli reassured his mother and, at the proper moment, sprang forth in a burst of light and cut off Coyolxauhqui's head and arms.

This is how she is portrayed on the stone, now displayed in the Templo Mayor Museum.

As was the custom, the Aztecs periodically enlarged Templo Mayor by simply building over the existing edifice. However, most of what remains to be seen is from the earlier constructions since the later construction was torn down and re-used by the Spanish during the Colonial Period.

A walk through the site of Templo Mayor helps one see the Aztec civilization as something more than isolated artifacts in a museum or as people who seem only to exist in history books.

Serpents, Eagles and Warriors

Templo Mayor was a sacred place. It was here that the Aztecs acknowledged the superiority of the gods and it was here that the debt was repaid to the gods for the gift of life. During a visit to Templo Mayor one can still sense that this place was special.

Throughout the site one can see examples of the various periods of construction. Also, in many areas there are large stone serpent heads as well as representations of huge serpents with undulating bodies. On one of the altars there are beautiful sculptures of frogs and, in an area known as the Eagle Knights Precinct, there are large carved eagle heads. Aztec warriors were divided into groups which associated themselves with the fierce qualities of animals such as the eagle and the jaguar. Stone benches with remnants of the original paint can also be seen in the Eagle Knights Precinct. This area is, unfortunately, covered by a protective roof and this makes it difficult to see and to photograph the multicolored designs on the benches.

Startling Faces from the Past

One of the most interesting sights at Templo Mayor is a group of eight stone statues which recline against a large staircase. The statues at the site are exact replicas of the originals which were found in this position. Each of the figures has a slightly different facial expression and, although the posture of each figure is rigid, the position of the hands and arms vary. Coming upon these figures, one has the startling impression that one has come face to face with a group of people from ages past.

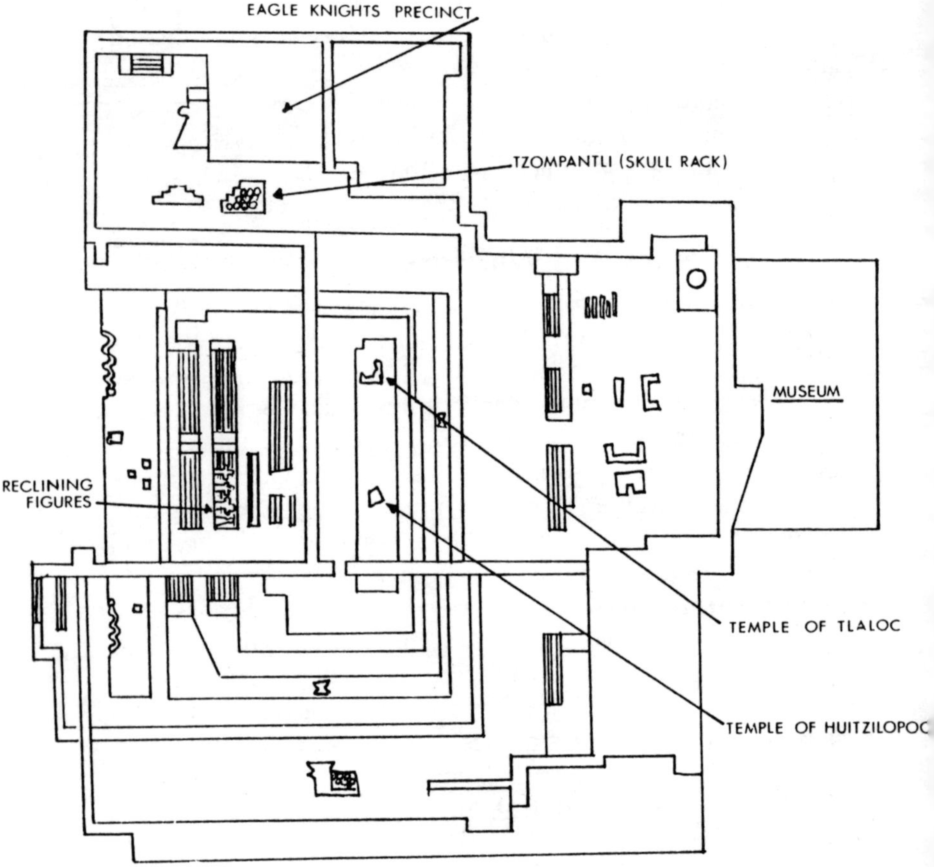

TEMPLO MAYOR

Temples of Human Offerings

The most sacred areas of Templo Mayor were the Temple of Tlaloc and the Temple of Huitzilopochtli. At the Tlaloc temple there is a multicolored Chac-mool, a reclining figure holding an offering dish over its abdomen, on which remnants of the original paint still can be seen clearly. In addition, many of the original designs which decorated the walls of both temples also remain.

It was here that offerings were made to Tlaloc, the god of rain, and to Huitzilopochtli, the Aztec sun god. The Aztecs knew that, as with all living things, rain and sun, in the proper proportions, were essential for survival. However, they also knew that too much or too little rain or sun could have devastating consequences. For the Aztecs, it was of vital importance to insure the continued favor of Tlaloc and Huitzilopochtli.

More Than Two Hundred Human Skulls

One of the most shocking sites at Templo Mayor is the Aztec skull rack known as a Tzompantli. This platform is made up of over two hundred human skulls which are covered with layers of plaster. These are the skulls of but a few who were sacrificed to the Aztec gods. The Tzompantli rarely fails to send a shiver through most visitors.

Some Hints

Most areas of Templo Mayor can be seen easily by visitors. However, one must view the site from walkways and it is impossible to get very close to certain areas. Details of the Eagle Knights Precinct, the Temple of Tlaloc and the Temple of Huitzilopochtli are best seen using binoculars or a telephoto lens.

The Newest Jewel in Mexico City's Crown

Newest of Mexico City's many museums, the Templo Mayor Museum is itself a work of art. Incorporated into the grounds of the archaeological site, the museum is built around a central atrium. Artifacts are displayed on four levels on either side of this court. The museum is designed to resemble the Great Temple which once stood but a few feet away. As visitors mount the stairs to the first four galleries, then descend through the next four, they have the impression of walking the twin staircases of Templo Mayor.

Photography, without flash, is allowed in the Templo Mayor

Museum. No permit is necessary. As in the Museum of Anthropology, high speed film should yield good results.

Gruesome but Interesting

Just beyond the entrance of the museum is a colorful and beautifully detailed model of Tenochtitlan as it looked during the time of the Aztecs. Even with a wide angle lens, however, it may be necessary to photograph this reproduction from one of the higher floors of the museum.

To the right, immediately preceding the stairs to Gallery 1, is a section from an Aztec skull rack. This is an excellent area for some interesting, though gruesome, close-up photography.

Unique Presentation

Throughout the building, illustrations and quotations are presented on illuminated, etched glass panels which further adds to the museum's uniqueness.

Antecedents/Beginnings—Gallery 1

The first gallery of the Templo Mayor Museum presents material and artifacts which relate to the early wanderings of the Mexica tribe. Since this group claimed that a place called Aztlan was their ancestral homeland, they were referred to as Aztecs (by the conquistadores), a name which has remained.

Among the many artifacts in Gallery 1 are a monumental stone carving of an eagle (which may have had some connection with the Eagle Knights), a model of Templo Mayor showing a cutaway view, a glass topographical map showing the distribution of the Mexicas throughout the Valley of Mexico, funerary offerings, sacrificial stone knives, and a monumental architectural embellishment in the form of a stylized snail.

War and Sacrifice—Gallery 2

The high point of Gallery 2, perhaps of the entire museum, is the monumental stone relief of the dismembered goddess Coyolxauhqui. The circular stone can be seen up close in this gallery, but can be appreciated more fully when one looks down upon it from Gallery 4.

Much of what was found in Templo Mayor consists of votive offerings. In one display case, an entire offering cache is exhibited as it was found in the temple. Skulls, jade and onyx pieces, and stone vessels bearing the image of Tlaloc appear to have been deliberately placed.

Farther along in the gallery is the magnificent onyx mask of Tecalli which appears to glow with an inner light. Nearby is a display of stone ceremonial knives which have a curiously skeletal quality because of their shell eyes and teeth. The next case contains a gruesome display of four human skulls, one of which has a stone ceremonial knife protruding from the nasal cavity. The eye sockets of the skulls are inlaid with eyes of shell.

Other important displays in Gallery 2 are a large case filled with wonderfully carved stone masks; the magnificent vessel bearing the image of Mictlantecuhtli, god of the dead; two exquisitely incised funerary urns, and a stone carved with the visage of Tlaltecuhtli, god of earth.

Tribute and Commerce—Gallery 3

The third gallery presents two of the major forces which helped to sustain the Aztec empire. Objects from various parts of Mexico found their way to Tenochtitlan and to the Templo Mayor via trade routes.

Gallery 3 displays huge braziers; jewelry, spear heads, and a club of obsidian; a Mixtec stone carving given as tribute; as well as gold, silver, and jade jewelry from what are today the Mexican states of Hidalgo, Puebla, Oaxaca, Guerrero, and Guanajuato.

The most striking object in this gallery is a jade mask carved in the style of Teotihuacan. The mask is inlaid with shell teeth and eyes.

The Monoliths—Gallery 4

Two life-size terracotta figures of Eagle Knights are the first artifacts one encounters in Gallery 4. The statues are magnificent in their detail and make excellent studies for full-figure or close-up photography. The figures stand upon carved and brightly-painted stone benches from the area of Templo Mayor known as the Eagle Knights Precinct.

A few feet away are a group of stone statues. Reproductions of these statues recline against a staircase in the Templo Mayor ruins.

Gallery 4 also exhibits a number of large braziers and monumental stone carvings. However, the most exciting aspect of the gallery is the unsurpassed view it affords of the stone of

Coyolxauhqui. Visitors gaze down at the circular monolity through an opening in the floor. Because of the size of the sculpture, a wide angle lens is necessary to photograph it in its entirety. For close-ups of the stone's details, a telephoto lens would yield good results. Binoculars are also very helpful in appreciating the artistry of this carving.

Tlaloc—Gallery 5

This gallery, from which one begins the descent through the rest of the museum, is dedicated to Tlaloc, god of water and fertility. Among the most interesting exhibits in this section is an offering cache containing masks, a boat, and a box with lid, all of stone.

The gallery also contains large sculptures, masks, small figures, and vessels, all of which relate to the worship of Tlaloc. Two of the most interesting objects in this area are two expertly carved squatting figures of Tlaloc, one of onyx and one of jade.

The high point of Gallery 5 is surely the blue and red polychromed vessel bearing the fanged image of Tlaloc. Fittingly, this object is suspended over an unusual fountain made of large, square pieces of glass placed one upon the other.

A more gentle side of the Aztec mentality can be seen in a delicately fashioned stone carving of a shell. This large sculpture, because of its relationship to water, is associated with the rain god, Tlaloc. As with all ancient Mesoamerican cultures, water played an important role in Aztec worship and this large sculpture is a confirmation of that role. The shell is one of two displayed in the museum.

Another interesting display in this gallery is a model of Aztec *chinampas* or floating gardens. Such areas made up a large part of Tenochtitlan.

Fauna—Gallery 6

Presented in this gallery are fish, birds, mammals, amphibians, reptiles, shells and corals which served an important role as offerings at the Great Temple.

Also, by mounting a small flight of stairs, visitors come to an area where they are looking down into an offering cache as if it were still *in situ*. Such innovative examples of architectural design help to give museum visitors a sense of discovery.

Religion—Gallery 7

Artifacts in this gallery relate to how the Aztecs viewed the universe. It presents the many facets of Aztec religion and the ceremonial objects connected with it. Exhibits in Gallery 7 are a portion of a platform with skull carvings, a brazier, jade and onyx pieces, ceremonial knives, and the second monumental stone sculpture of a shell.

The Conquest—Gallery 8

The final gallery of the Templo Mayor Museum deals with the arrival of the Europeans, an occurrence which would bring about the destruction of Tenochtitlan and change the face of Mexico forever.

Much of what is in this gallery is broken, illustrating the violence visited upon the Aztecs and their capital. Large fragments of monumental bas-reliefs are displayed along with small stone figures and masks. Also exhibited in this gallery are examples of gold jewelry found amid the ruins of the Great Temple.

The most unattractive piece in the entire museum is displayed in Gallery 8. It is a gold ingot. It symbolizes what was done not only to Aztec gold pieces, but to untold scores of golden masterpieces throughout the Americas. The gold was melted down, without regard to beauty or artistic merit, and cast into bars for easy transport to Europe.

Perhaps the most telling objects in this gallery are the great stones from Templo Mayor which have been recarved with Spanish designs. The conquerors literally put their stamp on what they had conquered.

A Treasury of Religious Art

Besides the National Museum of Anthropology, the Museum of the City of Mexico and Templo Mayor Ruins and Museum, Mexico City contains many sights and pleasures that are often overlooked. Two of these, the Metropolitan Cathedral and the National Palace, are located about one block from Templo Mayor.

The Cathedral and the Sagrario, a small church which adjoins it, are located on the Zocalo or Main Plaza of Mexico City. The facade of the Cathedral is highly ornamented and the huge interior contains numerous altars. The Cathedral and the Sagrario contain many fine examples of Mexican religious art.

Most Striking Murals in All of Mexico

Art of a different nature is found in the National Palace which stands on the east side of the Zocalo. It is here that Diego Rivera, one of Mexico's most renowned artists, painted some of his most impressive murals.

Above the main staircase, Rivera painted a series of ten interconnected murals known collectively as Mexico Through the Ages. The monumental work consists of *The Struggle of the Classes, The Legend of Quetzalcoatl, The Foundation of Tenochtitlan, The Conquest, The Colonial Epoch, The Mexican Independence, The American Intervention, The Reform Laws, The Execution of Maximilian,* and *The Mexican Revolution.*

In the corridor above the palace courtyard are nine additional murals of varying sizes: *The Great City of Tenochtitlan, The Tarascan Civilization, The Zapotec Civilization, The Totonac Civilization, The Rubber Tree, The Huaxtec Civilization, The Cacao Plant, The Maguey Plant,* and *The Arrival of Hernan Cortez to Veracruz.* This last mural was unfinished at the time of Diego Rivera's death in 1951.

The color and majesty of Mexico's ancient cultures, as well as events in Mexico's modern history, are presented in Rivera's works. His murals are visually powerful and are rightfully numbered among the treasures of Mexico's great artistic heritage.

Until recently, another of Rivera's most famous murals, *A Sunday Dream at the Alameda Park*, could be seen in the lobby of the Hotel Del Prado. Because of damage sustained in the earthquakes which occurred in 1985, the hotel is being demolished. Fortunately, the mural has been saved and moved to another location. Check locally as to whether it is once again on public exhibition.

Romantic Place for Lunch

Another of Mexico City's oft overlooked pleasures is directly across the Zocalo from the National Palace: the Hotel Majestic, one of the best hotels in the city. The hotel, whose entrance is at Avenida Madero 73, has a wonderful rooftop restaurant which overlooks the entire Zocalo. From the outside section of the restaurant one has spectacular views of the Cathedral, the Sagrario and the National Palace. This charming restaurant is one of the most romantic places in Mexico City.

Architectural Surprise

Although it is one of the most beautiful buildings in the world, the Palacio de las Bellas Artes is unfamiliar to many who visit Mexico City. The building exudes the romance of bygone eras, is one of Mexico City's most enjoyable sightseeing pleasures, and should not be overlooked. The Bellas Artes is located near Alameda Park at the corner of Avenida San Juan de Letran and Avenida Hidalgo.

Often simply referred to as the Bellas Artes, this architectural masterpiece incorporates a number of surprises into its design, and houses a theatre, a museum, a bookshop and a cafeteria.

The exterior of the Bellas Artes is in the Beaux Arts style yet incorporates design elements based on Aztec motifs. At various points on the exterior one can see the heads of Aztec jaguar warriors as well as those of coyotes and monkeys.

Unexpectedly, the interior of the Bellas Artes is one of the supreme examples of Art Deco. However, even more surprising is the use of Aztec and Mayan forms amid the geometric designs of this quintessential twentieth century decorative style. In the Grand Foyer there are three-story-high light fixtures crowned by masks of the Mayan rain god, Chaac, and the steel doors leading from this foyer into the theater bear stylized Aztec skulls of bronze.

Within the Bellas Artes one can also view works by some of Mexico's greatest artists. Among those represented are Diego Rivera, Rufino Tamayo and Jose Clemente Orozco.

A Meal In a Beautiful Colonial Building

Not far from the Bellas Artes is Sanborn's House of Tiles, one of the most pleasant places in Mexico City to have a meal. The restaurant, located at Avenida Madero 4, is in an enclosed inner courtyard in one of Mexico's most beautiful colonial structures. The building takes its name from the beautiful tiles (from the city of Puebla) which decorate its exterior.

Best Shop for Mexican Folk Art

A few steps from the House of Tiles, at Madero 10, hidden away in the rear of the building on the second floor, is Victor's, a shop which specializes in Mexican handicrafts. This shop is the best source for the finest quality *artes populares*, as handicrafts are termed in Mexico. Victor's is a shop for serious collectors and for those wishing to acquire something distinctively Mexican. Other branches of this shop can be found in Oaxaca and in Cancun.

Other good sources for *artes populares* in Mexico City are the National Museum of Popular Industrial Arts, at Avenida Juarez 44, and FONART, at Juarez 89, which are both run by the Mexican Government. You can find wonderful handmade wooden toys at this FONART.

A Refreshing Pause

For an excellent glass of beer, stop in at Restaurantes Americas which is right next door to the National Museum of Popular Industrial Arts. The beer is served in long glass beakers which arrive at your table supported by a wooden holder. Unless you have a large thirst (and even larger kidneys) do not ask for a *grande*, which stands about three feet tall.

Most Delicious Hot Chocolate in the City

For those interested in edible Mexican creations, Auseba is well worth a visit. Located at Hamburgo 159-B, in an area known as the Zona Rosa, Auseba serves delectable cakes and pastries as well as very rich hot chocolate. The decor is unpretentious and the staff is friendly. Auseba is one of Mexico City's special pleasures and it would be hard to find a more delightful place to spend some time relaxing after seeing the sights of Mexico City.

Shopping in the Zona Rosa

Many travelers to Mexico City tend to confine their shopping to the Zona Rosa. In general, prices are higher here than in other parts of the city.

Discriminating shoppers should, however, stop in at FONART, Los Castillo, and Coloniart.

Located at Londres 136-A, the Zona Rosa branch of FONART does not have as wide a selection as the one on Juarez. It is a good idea, though, to visit as many of these shops as possible, since they don't always carry the same items.

At Los Castillo, Amberes 41, some of the most beautiful silver pieces are for sale. This shop sells beaten silver vases (some inlaid with semiprecious stones), silver pitchers and serving plates, as well as silver jewelry.

Those interested in fine art from Mexico's colonial period should visit Coloniart at Estocolmo 37. The shop is a half-block in from Hamburgo, and features antique Puebla pottery, wooden chests, bronze candlesticks, original oil paintings, and carved wooden statues of saints known as *santos*.

A True Taste of Mexico

While in Mexico City, no one should miss experiencing Fonda El Refugio, a venerable restaurant serving authentic Mexican food in the Zona Rosa at Liverpool 166. Among the most delicious dishes are such appetizers as garnachas and nopalitos, and entrees like filete Fonda El refugio, chiles rellenos, and albondigas en chile chipotle. A cup of cafe de olla (coffee Mexican style), is a wonderful brew of coffee, brown sugar, cloves and cinnamon.

The Perfect Travel Destination

Because of its many special places, Mexico City offers a vast array of amenities and cultural experiences to the modern traveler. It is a city in which the exotic and the familiar often exist side by side. For those wishing the thrill of the exotic, but the security of the familiar, Mexico City is a perfect destination.

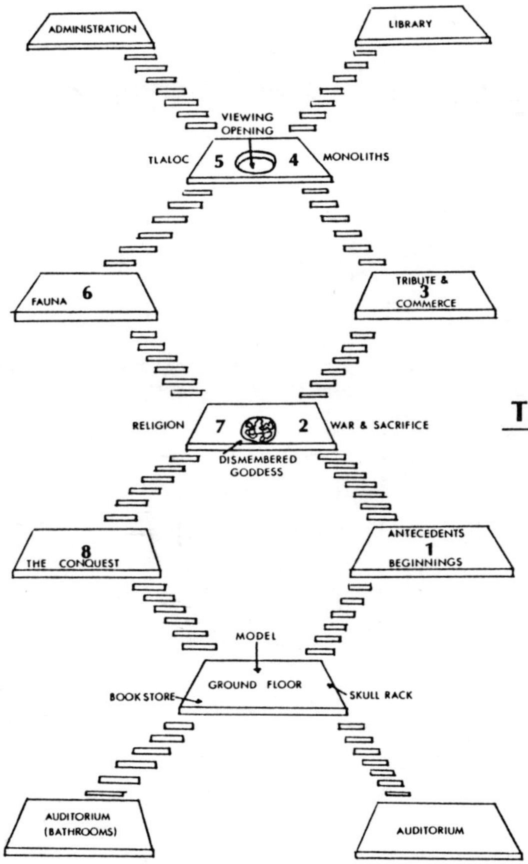

THE TEMPLO MAYOR MUSEUM

TEOTIHUACAN

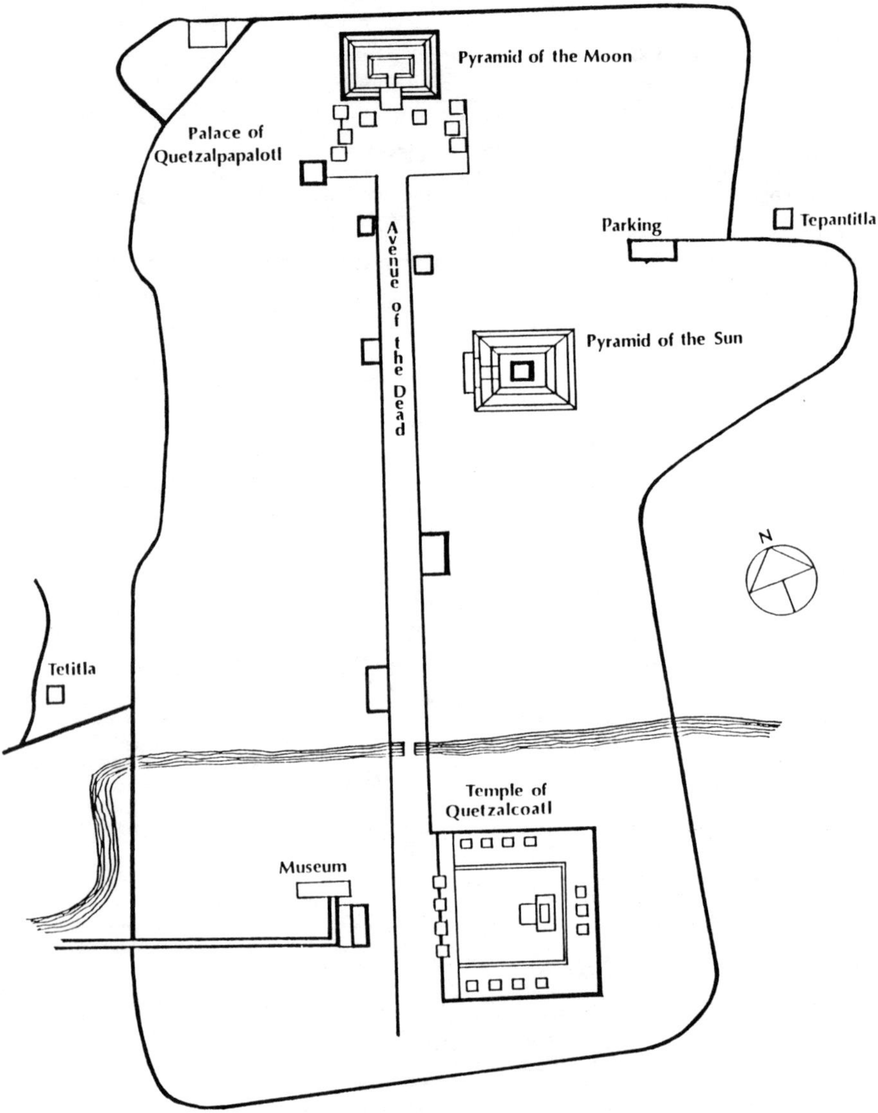

Chapter 2

TEOTIHUACAN

Where the Gods Came Down to Earth

Believed by the Aztecs to be the place where the gods sacrificed themselves to create the fifth sun, Teotihuacan is one of the most popular day trips from the capital and, as such, is probably one of Mexico's best known archaeological sites. Teotihuacan is open 9 a.m. to 5 p.m.

Many tour companies offer day trips to Teotihuacan and choices should be considered carefully. Since most of these tours also make stops at other attractions, time at the ruins is limited. With just a little effort, it is possible to reach Teotihuacan on one's own and at less expense. Simply take a No. 7 bus going north on Insurgentes to the Terminal Central de Autobuses del Norte. At the terminal look for the sign that reads Autobuses Teotihuacan. Doing so also affords an opportunity to see the site at an unhurried pace.

A Special Atmosphere

For those who truly wish to immerse themselves in the special atmosphere of Teotihuacan, it is possible to stay at a Villas Arqueologicas hotel just across from the site. The hotel, run by Club Med, has air-conditioned rooms which are tastefully furnished, a restaurant, a pool and tennis courts. Spending the night at Teotihuacan affords the time for a much more leisurely exploration of the ruins and it also affords the opportunity of seeing the Sound and Light show in the evening without the worry of having to get back to Mexico City.

Avenue of the Dead

Although abandoned long before the Aztec era, the Aztecs believed that Teotihuacan was a burial area for god-kings. The most important structures at Teotihuacan are clustered about the Avenue of the Dead, a broad, open expanse spanning the length of the site. This avenue affords visitors a convenient way to reach the major areas of interest. Not to be missed are the Pyramids of the Sun and the Moon, the Palace of Quetzalpapalotl, the Citadel and the Temple of Quetzalcoatl. Structures at Teotihuacan were named by the Aztecs, by the Spanish and by modern excavators.

Where Gods Came to Earth

Of all the structures at Teotihuacan, the Pyramid of the Sun dominates one's attention by its sheer mass. A climb to the summit is recommended not only for the view it affords but also for the contact it provides with the variety of people making their way up and down like ants on an elephant. Looking straight down the pyramid from the top provides another perspective on the massiveness of this structure. This is a wonderful place to contemplate the effort that went into building not only the pyramid but all of Teotihuacan. Standing on this spot one can believe that surely this was indeed a place where the gods came to earth. A person feels very small here and, looking down at the rest of Teotihuacan, one is awed knowing that mere humans created this monumental city.

Spectacular Overview

North of the Pyramid of the Sun stands the somewhat smaller Pyramid of the Moon, noteworthy for the beauty of its symmetry and also for the spectacular overview of Teotihuacan from its summit. The climb to the top is somewhat more difficult than that of the Pyramid of the Sun, but the effort is well rewarded with a view straight down the Avenue of the Dead and the structures which line it.

After descending the Pyramid of the Moon, time should be spent admiring the symmetry of the structures around the Plaza of the Moon in relation to the pyramid itself.

Special Place for Close-up Photography

Just off to one side of the Pyramid of the Moon stands the Palace of Quetzalpapalotl. By comparison, this building seems almost delicate after the monumentality of the two pyramids. At the top of the entrance stairway is an imposing serpent's head and inside the building is an atrium around which are four rooms. Mural remnants within this structure and the bas-reliefs on the columns of its atrium make the Palace of Quetzalpapalotl an excellent area for detail photographs.

Before visiting the Citadel and Temple of Quetzalcoatl, it is always pleasant to simply wander along the Avenue of the Dead. Flanking this broad, central avenue are interesting, though less imposing, structures such as the Temple of Mythological Animals, Temple of the Jaguar (which contains a beautiful mural), Palace of the Sun and Plaza of Four Little Temples. With guidebook in hand and surrounded by such grandeur, it is not difficult to imagine oneself in the ancient world of Teotihuacan.

Given its name by the Conquistadores, the Citadel may have contained the residences of Teotihuacan's priests and nobles. This series of platforms is strikingly plain in comparison to the nearby Temple of Quetzalcoatl.

Temple to a Serpent God

Though portions of the Temple of Quetzalcoatl are reproduced in full color in the National Museum of Anthropology nothing can compare with seeing the entire structure. Vibrant colors of its sculpture have faded over the centuries, but visages of ancient, mysterious gods are nonetheless powerful. Serpent heads jut out from the temple's sides along with carvings of an unknown god. There is nothing like the Temple of Quetzalcoatl, and once seen, it is never forgotten. Though named for the god Quetzalcoatl, some scholars feel that the representations are of an earlier serpent deity who, unlike Quetzalcoatl, was associated with water. These sculptures are arresting in their ferocity of expression and their beauty of execution.

After walking the length of this great city, one may wonder about its builders. Who were these Teotihuacanos? Little is known of them and what is known comes to us through archaeology. No written records mention Teotihuacan, and although glyphs have been found at the site, none has yet been deciphered. From archaeological evidence it seems that religion was an important and complex part of life for the Teotihuacanos, but scant knowledge exists of their gods or their myths.

Before leaving Teotihuacan, a visit to the museum is highly recommended. It is important to see the site as more than piles of stones and empty buildings having no relation to human living. The museum offers the visitor an insight into what is currently known about the inhabitants of Teotihuacan.

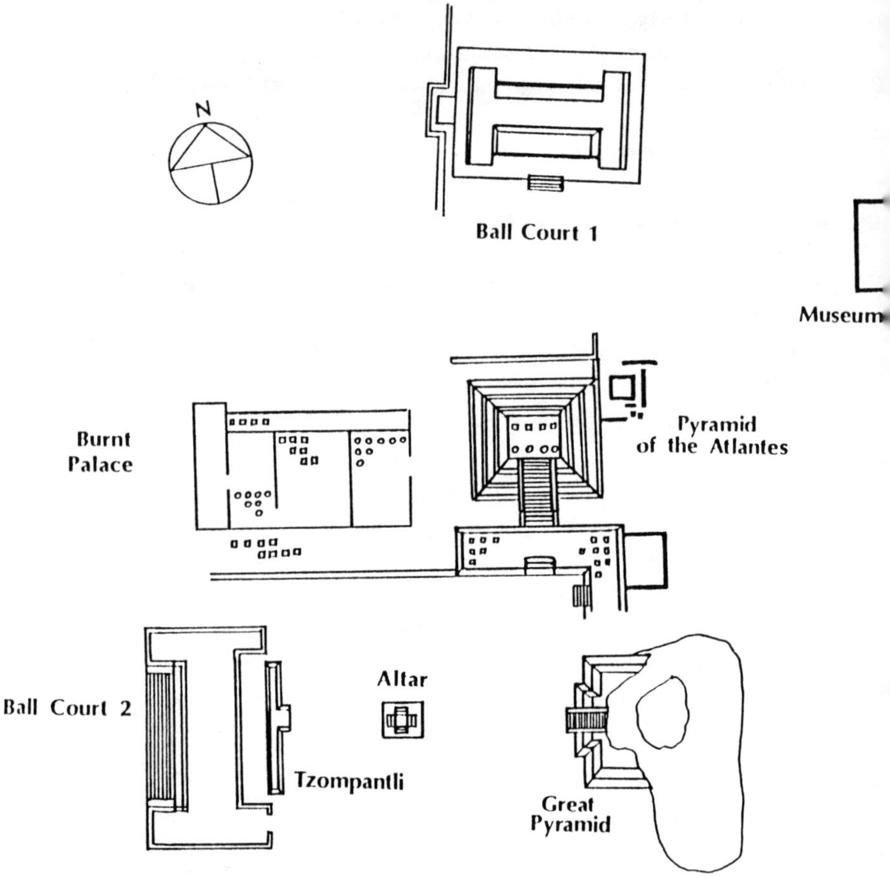
N
Ball Court 1
Museum
Burnt Palace
Pyramid of the Atlantes
Altar
Ball Court 2
Tzompantli
Great Pyramid

TULA

Chapter 3

TULA

(plus visits to Tenayuca and Santa Cecelia Acatitlan)

Giant Warriors of Stone

Once among the greatest cities of ancient Mexico, today little remains to attest to Tula's former magnificence. However, what does remain of the city gives the visitor interesting glimpses of its artistic achievements.

Tula (open 8 a.m. to 6 p.m.) is one of the most popular day trips from Mexico City and can be reached by tour bus or rental car. However, hiring a car with driver might be less expensive than taking a tour or using a rental car. It is also less frustrating and provides the opportunity to see more.

The Best Way to Visit Tula

Tours usually do not provide enough time to appreciate an archaeological site since stops are also often made at places which are of little interest. Furthermore, compared to what one gets, the tours are not a bargain.

Driving to Tula on one's own is not difficult once Highway 57 D is reached. However, driving through Mexico City to this road can be time-consuming and frustrating since street signs are often nonexistent. These problems can be avoided by hiring a driver and car.

Using a local driver not only helps to avoid problems but it also affords the opportunity to visit the small, but beautiful, sites of Tenayuca and Santa Cecelia Acatitlan. These ruins are on the way to Tula and, unfortunately, are not seen by most tourists. Both sites can be reached by rental car, but it is easy to get lost in the maze of streets leading to these ruins. Driving in Mexico City should be left to those who know the area. Arrangements to hire a driver can usually be made through one's hotel concierge.

What Most Tourists Never See

Combining visits to Tenayuca and Santa Cecelia Acatitlan with a visit to Tula is not only practical but interesting. Both Tenayuca and Santa Cecelia are believed to have been built by the

Chichimecs and later occupied and expanded by the Aztecs. It was also the Chichimecs who had destroyed the great Toltec city of Tula. The Aztecs greatly admired the Toltecs and were greatly influenced by their culture. They even went so far as to claim the Toltecs as their ancestors. Like the Chichimecs, the Aztecs adopted many Toltec architectural styles, and similarities can be seen when one visits all three sites.

Hundreds of Serpents

Tenayuca is only partially restored but its similarity to the Templo Mayor of Tenochtitlan is obvious. It is believed that the design of Tenochtitlan's major temple was based on that of Tenayuca's temple pyramid. Today, Tenayuca's most interesting aspects are its massive stairway and its serpents made of stone and mortar. Over one hundred serpents line the base of the pyramid on three sides. Originally there were hundreds more of these serpents and all were covered in stucco and brightly painted. On two sides of the pyramid, there are also two huge serpents whose bodies are coiled. These, too, are constructed of stone and mortar, but the heads are carved of stone. The summit of Tenayuca's pyramid affords interesting views of all the serpents.

One of a Kind

Approximately two miles north of Tenayuca, stands the only completely-reconstructed Aztec temple pyramid in all of Mexico. Today the structure takes its name from Santa Cecelia Acatitlan, a small town on the outskirts of Mexico City. The pyramid has a magnificent stairway and at the top stands a small temple, a stele and two stone-and-mortar braziers. Situated near the pyramid are a small garden and a museum. Placed throughout the garden are sculptures found at the site. The museum also contains a number of interesting artifacts. One of the most impressive of these is a skull rack which was connected with the rituals of human sacrifice.

Tenayuca and Santa Cecelia Acatitlan should be visited during the afternoon since both pyramids face west and are in the most flattering light at this time of day.

Tula should also be visited late in the day since its major structure, the Pyramid of the Atlantes, also faces west.

City of the Feathered Serpent

Before it was destroyed by the Chichimecs, Tula was a large and powerful city. It was founded by the great ruler Ce Acatl Topiltzin who added to his name that of the god Quetzalcoatl, the Feathered Serpent. Over the centuries, the stories of the ruler and the god became so intertwined that it is impossible to tell where fact ends and where myth begins. According to myth, Quetzalcoatl, man or god, tried to get his people to abandon the practice of human sacrifice. Because of this, he and his followers were eventually forced to leave Tula by an opposing faction which preferred a different god. Quetzalcoatl and his followers wandered throughout Mexico. They stopped at many places, including Cholula and Chichen Itza, and at each place Quetzalcoatl spread his beliefs. Eventually the wanderers came to the Yucatan where Quetzalcoatl taught the people many things. The people worshipped him and called him Kukulcan which in the Mayan language means Feathered Serpent. There are two versions of how Quetzalcoatl finally left his followers. One version states that Quetzalcoatl ascended to the heavens where he became Venus, the morning star. In another version of the myth, he sailed away over the ocean. In both versions Quetzalcoatl promised his people that he would one day return to them.

The Most Pervasive of Mexico's Myths

The story of Quetzalcoatl is, perhaps, the most important myth in Mexican culture. The myth, on its simplest level, portrays the conflict between rival tribal factions. On a more profound level, it represents the conflict between good and evil, between peaceful ways and violent ones. The myth is so elemental that is pervades not only Mexico's ancient art but its modern art as well.

It is sad that Tula, which is so strongly associated with the peace-loving Quetzalcoatl, met such a violent end. Today little remains of the city but, nonetheless, the site is interesting to visit.

Pyramid of Giant Warriors

The most interesting structure remaining at Tula is the Pyramid of the Atlantes. This structure is important because of magnificently-carved statues called "Atlantes" which grace the summit. These huge sculptures, which represent Toltec warriors, served as roof supports. The figures are known as Atlantes because in one hand they hold a weapon known as an atlatl.

Three of the Atlantes are original and one is a reproduction replacing a figure taken to the National Museum of Anthropology. The Atlantes are not carved from one solid block but consist of four sections. Behind the Atlantes are columns which contain beautiful bas-reliefs. Like the Atlantes, these columns are made up of four sections.

The east side of the Pyramid of the Atlantes also bears some beautiful bas-reliefs. These reliefs portray rows of jaguars as well as eagles eating hearts.

Other beautiful reliefs can be seen on Tula's famous Serpent Wall. The panels on this wall contain images of bones, serpents and human skulls. Some of the original paint can still be seen on these reliefs.

Violence Left Little Behind

In other areas of the site there are also some interesting painted reliefs but, in general, except for the Atlantes, little of Tula's art or architecture has survived. Tula's Great Pyramid, for example, is little more than a large mound. Its stairs have been restored but little else remains to be seen. However, from the top of the Great Pyramid one has a beautiful view of the Pyramid of the Atlantes.

Two of Tula's ball courts remain but they are in extremely poor condition. Ball Court Two is in a somewhat better state of preservation than Ball Court One, but neither compares with the ball court at Chichen Itza.

Tula also has a small museum which contains many of the artifacts found at the site. The artifacts are well displayed and the museum is an interesting way of beginning or ending a visit to Tula.

Even though Tula is not an extensive site, it is well worth a visit. The Toltec culture was influential in ancient Mexico and, if one is planning to visit other sites such as Chichen Itza, a visit to Tula affords insights which might otherwise be missed.

Chapter 4

PUEBLA and CHOLULA

Ancient Man-Made Mountain

Puebla is usually heralded as one of Mexico's most charming Colonial treasures. The city has a number of magnificent churches and buildings, many decorated with the Talavera tiles for which Puebla is famous. In spite of this, however, Puebla seems somehow dull and dreary.

Tourists who come to Puebla spend little time in the city. Usually a visit to Puebla is combined with one to the nearby ruins of Cholula and most tourists come to this area on a day trip from Mexico City. However, spending at least two full days in this region allows one to explore Puebla and the ruins of Cholula at an unhurried pace.

Accommodations and restaurants in Puebla are acceptable but none are truly wonderful. The best place to stay in the area is the Villas Arqueologicas Hotel at Cholula. The hotel's ambiance is beautiful and relaxing, the amenities are all one could ask for and the hotel's restaurant serves excellent food. The Cholula ruins are only a short walk from the hotel and Puebla is only eight miles away.

Puebla and Cholula can be easily reached from Mexico City by tour bus, by public transportation or by rental car. Although driving to the Puebla area on one's own affords more flexibility, such a drive does have some drawbacks.

A Beautiful but Dangerous Drive

For those who choose to drive, the best way to reach Puebla from Mexico City is via Highway 190 D, a toll road. However, driving through Mexico City can be extremely difficult. Streets are not well marked, traffic is usually heavy and it is not unusual to feel as if one is lost in a giant maze. Furthermore, during the afternoon, severe storms are often encountered on the trip between the two cities and it is also not uncommon for Zaragosa, the main road between Mexico City and Highway 190 D, to become heavily flooded.

Driving to Puebla is not without some rewards, however.

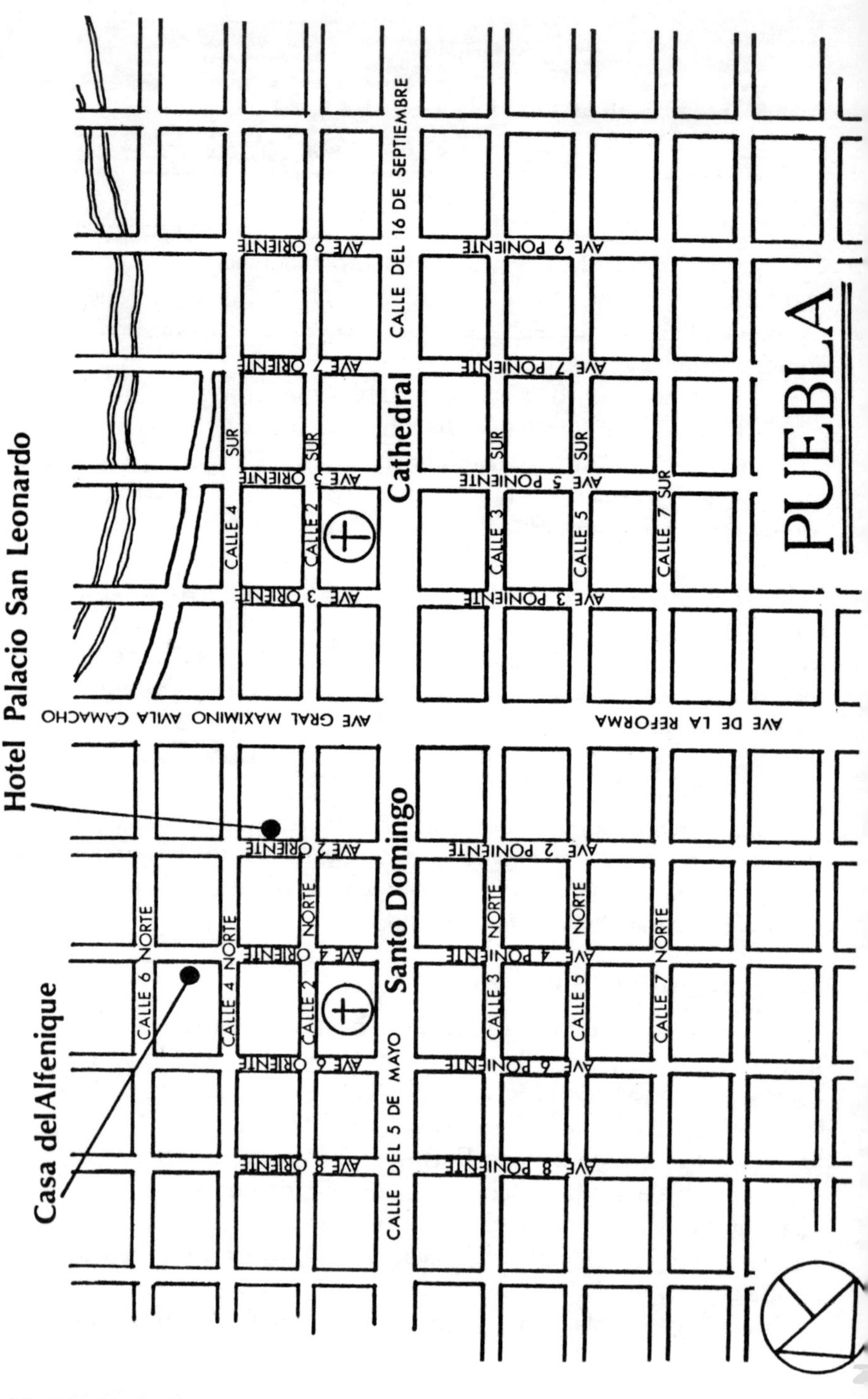

Hotel Palacio San Leonardo
Casa del Alfenique
Cathedral
Santo Domingo
PUEBLA
CALLE DEL 16 DE SEPTIEMBRE
CALLE DEL 5 DE MAYO
AVE GRAL MAXIMINO AVILA CAMACHO
AVE DE LA REFORMA
AVE 9 ORIENTE
AVE 7 ORIENTE
AVE 5 ORIENTE
AVE 3 ORIENTE
AVE 2 ORIENTE
AVE 4 ORIENTE
AVE 6 ORIENTE
AVE 8 ORIENTE
AVE 9 PONIENTE
AVE 7 PONIENTE
AVE 5 PONIENTE
AVE 3 PONIENTE
AVE 2 PONIENTE
AVE 4 PONIENTE
AVE 6 PONIENTE
AVE 8 PONIENTE
CALLE 4 SUR
CALLE 2 SUR
CALLE 3 SUR
CALLE 5 SUR
CALLE 7 SUR
CALLE 6 NORTE
CALLE 4 NORTE
CALLE 2 NORTE
CALLE 3 NORTE
CALLE 5 NORTE
CALLE 7 NORTE

Highway 190 D cuts through the mountains and the scenery is quite beautiful. As the road ascends, the landscape becomes rugged. The hills are covered with thousands of pine trees as well as a number of spectacular rock outcroppings.

As the highway descends from the mountains it passes by many small towns and villages. In many of the villages, homes are simple mud brick huts. In spite of the poverty, which is often shocking, TV antennas abound. One does pass industrialized areas on this highway but, in general, one is more likely to see fields of corn, horses and sheep grazing peacefully, and farmers using burros to till their land.

A Magnificent Old Residence

In Puebla, the Casa del Alfenique, the cathedral and the Church of Santo Domingo, with its magnificent Rosary Chapel, comprise three of the city's most interesting sights.

The Casa del Alfenique is an eighteenth century residence which houses a small regional museum. Beautiful period furnishings are displayed throughout the house along with a few pre-Hispanic artifacts. However, the most interesting feature of the Casa del Alfenique is its traditional Mexican kitchen containing numerous utensils and ceramic cooking pots.

Another aspect of Mexican culture can be appreciated by visiting some of Puebla's churches. Besides their religious and historical significance, they are also important as repositories of some of Mexico's most beautiful works of art.

Whimsical Wooden Carvings

One of Puebla's most interesting churches is its huge cathedral. This massive structure is partially enclosed by an interesting fence consisting of stone columns connected by bronze grillwork. Upon each of the columns stands an angel which holds a light bulb in its raised hand. Within the connecting grillwork, the image of an eagle with a serpent in its beak is frequently repeated. This image, which is the symbol of Mexico, is seen repeatedly in numerous works of art throughout the country. The cathedral's interior is most impressive for its main altar and its huge choir. The domed main altar contains large marble statues of angels and saints which surround its focal point, a gold encrusted statue of the Virgin Mary. Equally beautiful are the carved figures of the choir. More impressive than the sheer mass of the choir, these carvings add a whimsical note to this rather somber church. Cherubs support the pipes of the great organ and peering out from between these pipes are angels playing various musical instruments.

The Most Breathtaking Interior in Puebla

Although it is smaller than the cathedral, the Church of Santo Domingo is far more impressive. The interior of the church is magnificently decorated. The main altar, for example, is a gilded masterpiece containing statues of angels and saints. However, even this breathtaking altar pales next to Santo Domingo's Rosary Chapel. Because of the vast amounts of gold leaf used within this chapel, it seems to radiate light. The ceiling and upper walls are gilded and a domed, golden altar enshrines a statue of the Virgin. Interestingly, there is a touch of whimsy in this otherwise reverential chapel. The lower portion of the walls are decorated with tiles bearing images of chubby-faced cherubs.

Where to Purchase World Famous Tiles

Throughout Puebla one sees countless examples of the decorative tiles for which the city is famous. These tiles are sold throughout the world but are far less expensive if bought in Puebla. Three of the best shops specializing in these tiles are La Trinidad, Casa Rugerio and Uriarte.

La Trinidad, located at Avenida 20 Poniente 305, does not have an extensive selection of tiles but it does have a good selection of faience bowls, dishes and cups.

Casa Rugerio has a large selection of tiles and prices are very reasonable. Service is very good in this shop and customers are not pressured to buy. The shop is located at Avenida 18 Poniente 111.

Of the three shops mentioned, Uriarte has the most extensive collection of tiles and faience pieces. Located at Avenida 4 Poniente 911, prices at this shop are higher than at the other two but Uriarte does accept credit cards.

How to Buy Tiles

When purchasing tiles a few things should be kept in mind. One should know the exact measurements of the area one plans to cover with the tiles. It is also a good idea to bring along a tape measure because tiles come in different sizes. Since prices and designs vary from shop to shop, it is also a good idea to compare prices before making a purchase. If the tiles are going to be used to form a pattern, one should figure out how many tiles of each type will be needed. One should also buy approximately ten percent more tiles than one needs to allow for any breakage which can occur during travel. Although Puebla's tiles are magnificent, it should not be forgotten that they are a heavy item to carry around for the rest of one's trip.

A Place for a Relaxing Meal

Those wishing to relax after shopping and sightseeing might want to try the restaurant in the Hotel Palacio San Leonardo which is located at Avenida 2 Oriente 211. The restaurant serves good food and prices are extremely reasonable.

A Tropical Surprise

The best place for relaxation in this area is, of course, Club Med's Villas Arqueologicas Hotel at Cholula. Virtually identical to Club Med's hotels at Teotihuacan, Uxmal, Chichen Itza and Coba, it is a small, self-contained resort. The hotel is built around a swimming pool and all rooms are air-conditioned. The numerous tropical trees and flowering plants add to the relaxing atmosphere of the hotel. Bougainvillea climbs the walls, banana trees stretch skyward and sweet peas, calla lilies and geraniums brighten the hotel's grounds with their colorful flowers. In addition to the hotel's tropical setting, there are subtle reminders that one is only a short walk from an important archaeological site. Incorporated into the hotel's design are glass enclosed niches which contain reproductions of pre-Hispanic artifacts.

The Big Attraction

A short distance from the hotel are the ruins (open 10 a.m. to 5 p.m.) which attract visitors to Cholula. Little reconstruction has been done and the site's major structure, the Great Pyramid, lies under a mound of earth and vegetation. Nonetheless, one cannot help being impressed at Cholula. The mound is massive in size and it is exciting to try to imagine what the pyramid looked like in ancient times. Unfortunately, the Great Pyramid will probably always be hidden from view since it is doubtful that it could ever be fully restored. Most of the pyramid was built of adobe bricks and these, for the most part, have so deteriorated over the centuries that reconstruction will probably never be possible.

Quetzalcoatl's Pyramid

The Great Pyramid was dedicated to the god Quetzalcoatl. Cholula was an important religious center and pilgrims came to it from great distances to honor Quetzalcoatl. The pyramid was built around the time of Christ and was added to for approximately eight centuries. Some scholars believe that Cholula was abandoned sometime during the eighth century A.D. However, little is known about how the city met its end and much that has come down to us about Cholula is shrouded in myth. One of the most famous myths from Cholula concerns Ce Acatl Topiltzin Quetzalcoatl. It said that after he and his followers were expelled from Tula they spent a period of time in Cholula before they continued their wanderings. While in the city, Quetzalcoatl taught the people many things and was much beloved by them.

Two areas at the base of the Great Pyramid have been reconstructed and give some idea of Cholula's former beauty. The Patio of the Altars contains wide stairs, stelae, fretwork designs and four altars. Nearby, protected by glass, are a few skeletal remains. A short distance from the Patio of the Altars is the Stone Building which is on the west side of the Great Pyramid. The Stone Building is beautifully restored and helps one to imagine the full magnificence of the Great Pyramid.

The New Order and a Floating Church

Climbing to the top of the Great Pyramid also adds to one's appreciation of the size of this structure. Standing atop this great mound one has a view of the countryside for miles around. During colonial times a church was erected on top of the pyramid mound. Its location is symbolic of what happens when one culture conquers and dominates another. This process had taken place numerous times before the Spanish had ever set foot in the New World. The Spanish were Mexico's last conquerors but, unlike previous conquerors, they not only brought with them a new God but refused to accept the existence of any other gods.

At night the church atop the Great Pyramid is illuminated and, in the darkness, the mound seems to disappear and the church appears to float in mid-air.

A short distance from the Great Pyramid is a small museum. The most interesting feature of the museum is its model of the Great Pyramid and the surrounding structures which once existed. The model also shows the pyramid in cross-section which gives some idea of earlier construction phases.

Both Cholula and Puebla can add to one's enjoyment of Mexico and, although activities and sightseeing are somewhat limited, a visit to this area of Mexico can be a welcome change of pace.

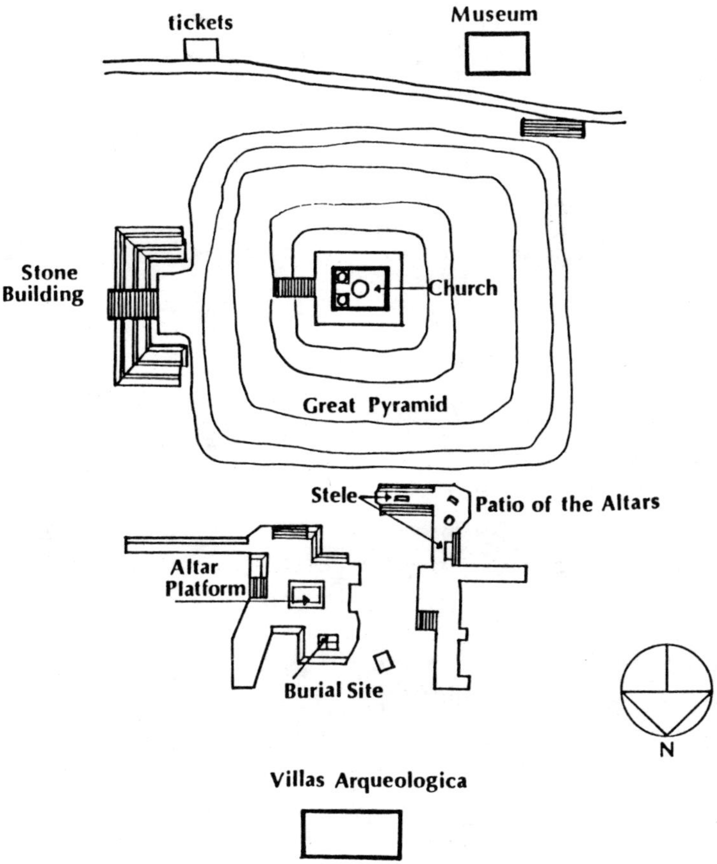

CHOLULA

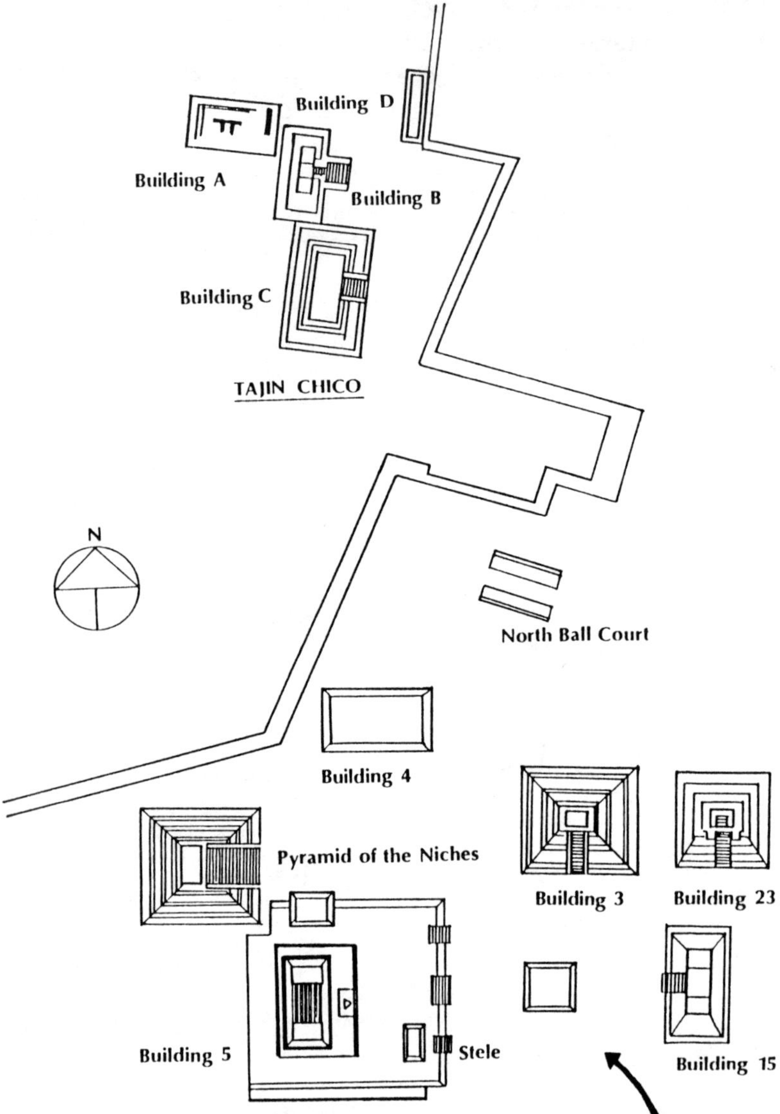
Building D
Building A
Building B
Building C
TAJIN CHICO
N
North Ball Court
Building 4
Pyramid of the Niches
Building 3
Building 23
Building 5
Stele
Building 15
South Ball Court

EL TAJIN

Chapter 5

EL TAJIN

The Unsolved Mystery

There is no question that El Tajin is one of Mexico's major archaeological treasures. There is also no question that very few travelers ever visit this magnificent site. El Tajin is in Veracruz State, an area of Mexico that has not been greatly developed for tourism. Although the ruins are spectacular and the surrounding area is lush and exotic, there is little else in the region to interest most tourists.

Where the Tour Buses Never Go

El Tajin is not extremely difficult to reach but it does require more effort to visit than Mexico's other major archaeological sites. Until recently, the easiest way to reach this region was by air. However, all scheduled flights to Poza Rica, the nearest airport to the ruins, have been canceled. Since Aeromexico frequently revises its flight schedule, air service to Poza Rica may be reinstated. Check with the airline.

Many travelers are reluctant to visit this region of Mexico because English is not commonly spoken in this part of the country and because the available amenities are not what most tourists are willing to accept.

Where to Stay

Those who visit this area of Mexico usually choose to stay in the small town of Papantla as opposed to staying in Poza Rica which is highly industrialized.

If you hire a taxi in Papantla to take you to the ruins of El Tajin, be sure that the taxi driver understands that he is to wait for you at the ruins for the return trip to Papantla.

Papantla is an unhurried little town which allows visitors the opportunity to experience an area of Mexico which still retains most of its local character.

It is difficult to rent a car in this area. However, cars can be rented in Mexico City or Veracruz for the drive to the El Tajin ruins. From Mexico City, it is possible to reach the ruins by car via

MEX 130 in approximately five hours. From Veracruz, the ruins can be reached, via MEX 180 in approximately four hours. Papantla can be reached from these cities by bus. If one has not arrived in Papantla via rental car, one can hire a driver with car to reach the ruins of El Tajin.

The steep mountain roads between Poza Rica can be extremely dangerous. They have sharp curves and do not have guardrails. Those driving in this area should exercise extreme caution.

The Exoticism of Ancient Ways

In Papantla, one is more apt to see goods being carried upon the back by means of a head strap, as the ancients did, or being carried upon the head rather than in the arms. It is also not unusual to see Totonac Indians in this city. Totonac men and women wear billowing white shirts and pants and go about their business with great dignity.

Although much of what one sees in Papantla is wonderfully exotic, the city's accommodations are barely acceptable. The best the city has to offer, the Hotel El Tajin, is rather dreary and disappointing. However, the view of Papantla from this hotel's upper, front stories is lovely.

Delicious but Inexpensive Meals

Accommodations in Papantla may not be the best but some excellent and inexpensive meals can be enjoyed in the city. The best restaurant in Papantla, the Terraza Cafe, overlooks the Zocalo. The restaurant's entrance and sign are in an alley and can, therefore, be missed. However, the restaurant's terrace can be easily spotted and finding the entrance is then easy. The Terraza Cafe offers excellent shrimp dishes. Among the best are camarones al mojo de ajo, for those who like a garlic sauce, camarones enchilados which has a hot chili sauce, and camarones a la pimienta which is made with fried peppers and onions. Also quite good are the enchiladas Suizas which are made with chicken and cheese. Bocoles Rellenos, corn cakes made with beans and cheese or ham, are also very tasty. The staff at the Terraza Cafe is helpful and courteous but does not speak any English.

A Sculpture and Flying Men

Other than enjoying meals at the Terraza Cafe, there is little else to do in Papantla. The market sells the beautiful white clothing worn by the Totonacs but little else would interest most travelers. The most impressive sights in Papantla are the giant bas-relief and the performances by the voladores. The bas-relief, which can be seen from the Zocalo, portrays, on a grand scale, numerous Totonac motifs. The central image of the relief is the Pyramid of the Niches at El Tajin. The voladores are men who perform from the top of a high pole which is in front of the cathedral. Performances are held on Sundays and holidays. Tied to ropes by their feet, four voladores spin ever-closer to the ground to the music of a fifth man seated atop the pole. The performance is rooted in antiquity and is thought to be related to ancient myth or to represent the passage of time as calculated by the ancients.

Smartest Way to Reach El Tajin Ruins

The major reason for being in Papantla is, of course, its proximity to the ruins of El Tajin which are open 9 a.m. to 5:30 p.m. daily. To reach these ruins it is best to hire a car with driver for a few hours. This can be easily done in Papantla. Approximately three hours should be allotted to reach the site, to explore the ruins and to return to Papantla. It is essential that the driver understands that he is to wait at the ruins. There are no taxis at the site. No tour buses go to the ruins and, by public transportation, it is necessary to take two buses to make the trip between Papantla and El Tajin. For the few dollars it takes to hire a car and driver, one has the security of knowing one will be able to get back to Papantla.

Best Time of Day

The ruins of El Tajin are best visited in the early morning. It is coolest at this time of day and since El Tajin's most famous structure, the Pyramid of the Niches, faces east, this is the best time to photograph it.

Most Mysterious Pyramid in Mexico

The Pyramid of the Niches is one of the most unusual of Mexico's ancient structures. The pyramid contains over three hundred niches which are believed to serve a solely decorative purpose. However, it has been speculated that the niches may represent the three hundred and sixty-five days of the year and that the entire design of the pyramid may have had a religious significance. Whatever motive lay behind the design of this structure, it is one of the most impressive architectural creations in the world.

Builders Unknown

A short distance southeast of the Pyramid of the Niches is a structure known as Building Five. This massive structure is most noted for the large sculpture which stands in front of its staircase. This monolithic carving may represent a death god or Tajin, the Totonac thunder god. However, El Tajin was not built by the Totonacs, as was previously thought, but by an earlier, unknown people.

Ball Game and Blood Sacrifice

The south side of Building Five also makes up one side of the South Ball Court. This court should not be overlooked because of the beautiful bas-reliefs it contains. These reliefs are exquisitely carved and reveal a great deal about the culture responsible for the creation of El Tajin. The reliefs clearly portray human sacrifice, self-mutilation, and various aspects of the ritual ball game played in this court. The player's gear can be seen plainly and it is similar to stone objects found in the area of El Tajin and throughout the state of Veracruz. It had been thought that the stone objects were actually worn during the games. However, their weight makes this hard to believe. The stone yokes which have been found, for example, are large, intricately carved horseshoe-shaped objects which were thought to have been worn around the waist. It is now thought that the stone objects simply represented those made of wood or leather. However the games were played, their gruesome aspects are quite evident in the bas-reliefs of the South Ball Court.

The main area of El Tajin contains a number of other structures. In front of Building Five, for example, is a large stone platform referred to as an altar. Nearby stand Buildings Three and Twenty-three. Both are massive stepped structures. They now bear little ornamentation but Building Three does have remnants of its original blue paint. Building Fifteen is also in this area and from its summit one has good views of the other structures in this area of El Tajin. Furthermore, Building Fifteen, though not completely restored, bears niches similar in design to those of the Pyramid of Niches.

An Area Few Know About

From the main section of El Tajin, a path leads to another area known as Tajin Chico. The structures in this area were constructed at a later date than those of the main area. For this reason, and because the area is far less restored than the main area, it is called Tajin Chico or Little Tajin.

The path leading to Tajin Chico passes the North Ball Court which is not as well preserved as the South Ball Court. However, the North Ball Court does have two beautiful bas-reliefs. The other reliefs in this ball court are, unfortunately, in poor condition.

A Bent Index Finger

Beyond the North Ball Court, five structures comprise Tajin Chico. Building A bears beautiful bent cross designs and Building B has niches similar to those found on other structures at this site. One of the most impressive structures at Tajin Chico is Building C which is noted for the designs found in its niches. These designs resemble a bent index finger and have been compared to designs created by the ancient Greeks. Also of some interest is Building D. Though not well preserved, this structure bears beautiful geometric stucco designs. Nearby is the Hall of the Columns which is also not well preserved. In an effort to protect the intricately carved columns, for which this structure has been named, they have been moved to an area near the El Tajin Museum.

Fragments of a Once Great City

The El Tajin Museum is located near the entrance to the site. The carved pillars from the Hall of the Columns can be found, under a protective metal roof, just outside the small museum. Housed within the museum are fragments of relief carvings and architectural details which were found throughout the area of El Tajin.

Mystery Continues

Although the beauty of El Tajin is obvious to all who behold it, most of its past remains a mystery. At its height El Tajin was an important and influential city. It had contact with a number of other important pre-Hispanic cultures but, in general, little is known about El Tajin, the people who built it or how the city met its end. Some have speculated that the city was ritually burned by its own inhabitants. Others believe that, like the great cities of Teotihuacan and Tula, El Tajin was invaded and destroyed by the Chichimecs.

For the modern visitor, El Tajin's mysterious past adds to the site's allure. One cannot help wanting to know more about the culture which gave rise to this impressive city. Most visitors to Mexico, however, never venture to El Tajin. This is unfortunate but understandable. Hopefully, in the future, more attention will be paid to tourism in this area. For the present, the ruins of El Tajin will be seen only by the few travelers willing to make the extra effort it requires to reach this site.

Chapter 6
OAXACA
Exotic Indian Homeland

Long a center of Indian culture, Oaxaca is one of the most interesting travel destinations in the world, offering the visitor a wide variety of experiences. Most who come to Oaxaca do so to see the fabled ancient cities built by the Zapotecs and Mixtecs. These cities, though now in ruins, still have the power to inspire awe in the modern visitor. Besides these archaeological treasures there are a multitude of other attractions in and around Oaxaca City, capital of the state of the same name. Among them are numerous colonial buildings, Indian markets, nearby villages offering a variety of handicrafts, shops filled with wonderful buys, and two exceptional museums.

Leaving the Airport

After arriving at the Oaxaca airport, it is a fairly short and inexpensive trip to the center of town via *colectivos*. Except for rental cars, these small vans are the only way of getting to town since taxis are not allowed to solicit passengers at the airport.

The Most Exceptional Hotel in Oaxaca

For those wishing to experience the atmosphere of Mexico's Colonial past, there is no finer place to stay in Oaxaca City than the El Presidente Ex Convento. Once a convent, this hotel has been carefully converted to modern use while remaining faithful to the period architecture. Throughout the building one can see fragments of murals which are mute testament to a long gone era in which the Catholic Church exerted a much stronger influence throughout Mexico than it does today. As one walks through the corridors of this former convent, it is enchanting to see the faces of angels and saints peering down from walls and ceilings. The hotel contains a number of flower-filled court yards as well as a swimming pool. Stepping into the El Presidente one feels transported to the tranquility of another time and place. Furthermore, the El Presidente offers a wonderful breakfast buffet each morning as well as an exceptional Sunday buffet featuring regional food.

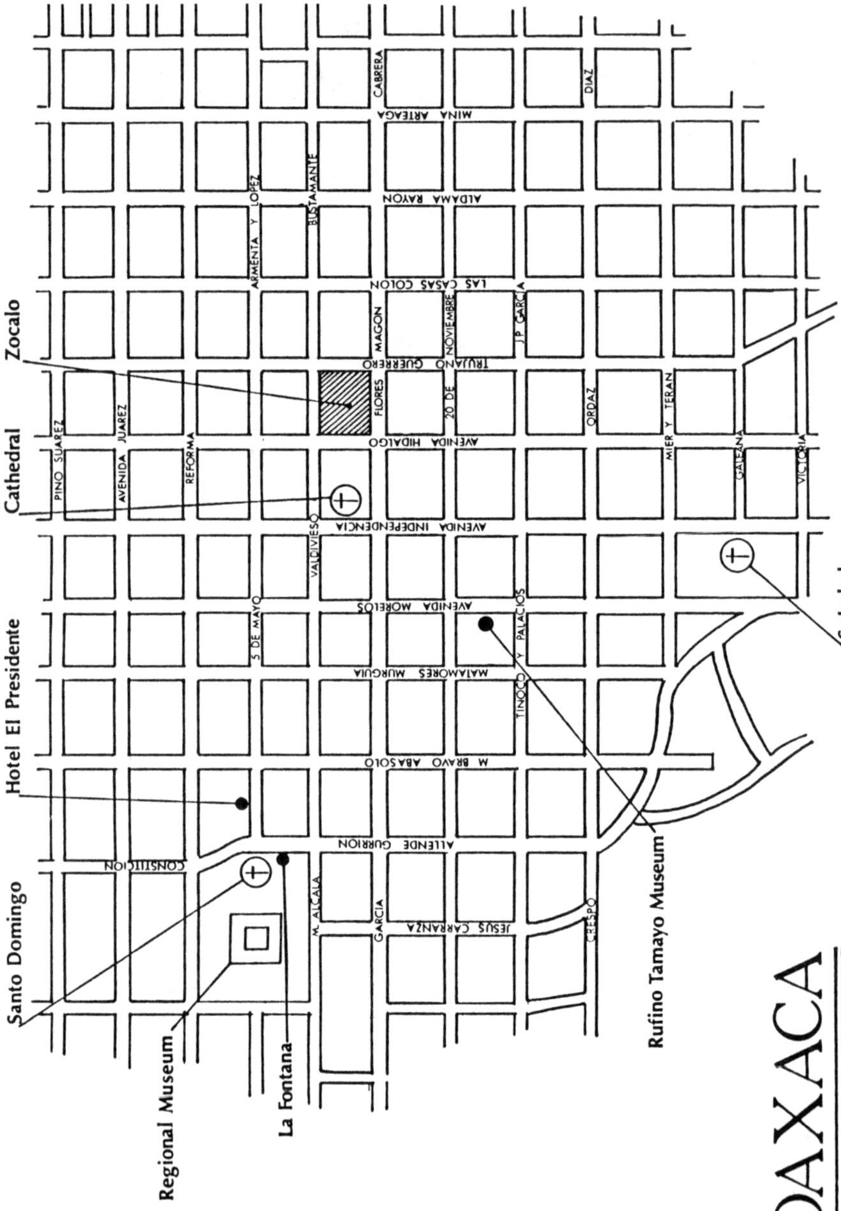
OAXACA
Zocalo
Cathedral
Hotel El Presidente
Santo Domingo
Regional Museum
La Fontana
Rufino Tamayo Museum
Soledad
MINA ARTEAGA
ALDAMA RAYON
LAS CASAS COLON
TRUJANO GUERRERO
AVENIDA HIDALGO
AVENIDA INDEPENDENCIA
AVENIDA MORELOS
MATAMORES MURGUIA
M BRAVO ABASOLO
ALLENDE GURRION
CONSTITUCION
JESUS CARRANZA
PINO SUAREZ
AVENIDA JUAREZ
REFORMA
ARMENTA Y LOPEZ
5 DE MAYO
BUSTAMANTE
VALDIVIESO
M. ALCALA
CABRERA
FLORES MAGON
GARCIA
20 DE NOVIEMBRE
J.P. GARCIA
TINOCO Y PALACIOS
DIAZ
ORDAZ
CRESPO
MIER Y TERAN
GALEANA
VICTORIA

Oaxaca's Finest Food

Considered by many to be the best restaurant in Oaxaca City, La Fontana is less than half-a-block from the El President. Food is cooked in an open kitchen and it is entertaining to watch one's meal being prepared. The food at La Fontana is inexpensive and exceptionally good, and the service is prompt and friendly.

Food for the Spirit

For those wishing food for the spirit, there are two churches a short distance from the El Presidente which typify the architecture, craftsmanship and religious devotion of Mexico's colonial period.

A Church Which Should not be Missed

The most spectacularly decorated church in Oaxaca City, Santo Domingo, is vibrant with color and detail. The ceiling of the church is richly ornate, the most famous section being just above the entrance. Amid a profusion of carved and painted leaves and branches, there appear human portraits. These small bas-reliefs represent the family tree of Saint Dominic for whom the church is named. The main altar of the church is also highly decorated as is the Chapel of the Rosary. The candles reflecting off the gilding of this chapel give it a warm, other worldly glow.

Oaxaca's Special Virgin

The Basilica de la Soledad impresses in a different way. Although the facade is highly embellished with columns and statues of saints, the interior is fairly plain. The focal point of this church, and of local devotion, is the statue of the Virgin of Solitude. The statue is dressed in a gold embroidered black velvet robe and stands above the main altar. The Virgin of Solitude is the patroness of the City of Oaxaca and reproductions of the statue, made of the distinctive black pottery of the area, can be found in shops throughout the city.

World Famous Indian Market

Oaxaca's Indian market is a more earthbound experience but is nonetheless a delight for those whose sense of adventure leans toward the exotic. Every Saturday the Indians, more properly called indigenous people, hold this market to buy and sell goods.

The market covers a large area on the outskirts of the city and offers a seemingly infinite variety of goods for sale. Fruits, vegetables, spices, textiles, clothing, rope, baskets, pottery, livestock, almost anything one could need can be found at this market. In recent years its fame has spread, and it has become somewhat of a tourist attraction. The market is not totally overrun with tourists and one can still enjoy the exoticism it offers. However, this market does seem more structured than in the past, and it is so crowded that it is often difficult to navigate through it.

A Market Few Outsiders Ever See

For an almost totally unspoiled market, one should visit the village of Ocotlan which holds its market on Friday. Ocotlan is only twenty miles from Oaxaca City and its market is less touristed than the one in Oaxaca. At Ocotlan one has more of a feeling of having stepped back in time to an authentic pre-Columbian marketplace. Like their ancestors, the people dress in colorful, hand-loomed garments and most sit quietly upon the ground with their wares spread before them on large pieces of cloth. Few sellers call out to prospective buyers, but when they do, it is always done in warm and friendly tones.

Turkeys and chickens, their feet tied, look calmly about as they are carried in large flat baskets upon the heads of women. Here, too, are a myriad of spices, fruits, vegetables, meat, textiles and cooking utensils. Almost anything one could want or need can probably be found at this market.

The market fills the main square and spills over into adjoining areas. To shade people from the sun, large sheets of cloth are suspended over a good deal of the main square so that the market looks as if it is taking place under one great canopy.

Live Goods

A few dusty streets away from the central market, there is a livestock market where goats, sheep and pigs are for sale. Although this market is not colorful, and it does take place amid dirt and mud, it is unusual. For those unfamiliar with livestock, it is fascinating to see a large sow reclining in the mud, suckling her piglets or to see a ewe nursing her lamb.

Little Affected by Outside World

Unlike the Oaxaca market that of Ocotlan seems little affected by the outside world and somehow seems to be about the business of living in a way that modern shopping malls never do. At Ocotlan the Indians are not preoccupied with display for its own sake and the market does not look like a theatrical set. The people take pride in their wares and are genuine in their concern for their customers.

Other villages of note in the area of Oaxaca City are Teotitlan del Valle and San Bartolo Coyotepec. Each of these villages is famed for a different handicraft and is an interesting side trip from Oaxaca City.

Best Area for Purchasing Unique Rugs

Teotitlan del Valle is noted for its weaving. Unusual rugs of varying quality and price ranges can be purchased in this village. Many of the rugs made in this village bear designs based on the cut stone fretwork designs which can be seen at the nearby ruins of Mitla. It is also possible to commission a special design and one can even watch the weaving being done. Friendly bargaining is expected, but one should not ask prices or begin to bargain unless one is serious about buying something. The concept of window shopping does not apply here. Teotitlan del Valle is probably the best place in the area to buy rugs. The craftspeople of this village take great pride in their work and what one pays for is what one gets.

Buyers Beware

This is not always the case when buying rugs at markets in Oaxaca, Ocotlan or Mitla. Buyers should be sure that if they are paying for a woolen rug, they are, in fact, getting one made of wool. For those who are unfamiliar with textiles or if any doubts arise, the best option is simply not to buy. Those intent on owning a beautiful Zapotec rug are well advised to travel the fourteen miles from Oaxaca to Teotitlan del Valle.

Oaxaca State's Unique Pottery

Noted for its distinctive black pottery, the village of San Bartolo Coyotepec is only seven miles from Oaxaca City. Although this pottery can be purchased in shops throughout Oaxaca, it is interesting to visit San Bartolo because one can often see demonstrations of how the pottery is made. True to ancient ways, the pottery is made without the use of a potter's wheel. The most famous potter in San Bartolo was Dona Rosa, and although she died a few years ago her family still produces pottery at her studio which is open to the public. Blackware will not hold water but those with a gray coloration will. Choices should be made accordingly.

More Distinctively Mexican Creations

Those with a further interest in handicrafts, known as *arte popular*, will be pleased with the wide selection in Oaxaca's shops. Offered for sale are pottery, painted tin ornaments, tin framed mirrors, various objects made of hand hammered copper, hand-blown glassware, corn husk dolls, handwoven textiles and clothing, silver and gold jewelry, carved wooden furniture, wooden masks, and hand carved wooden animals painted in fanciful colors.

Masterpieces in Wood

The best of these whimsical animals are created by Manuel Jimenez and his sons, Angelico and Isaias. The work of Señor Jimenez has been exhibited in a number of museums and his animals can sometimes be found in shops such as Victor's. However, Señor Jimenez does not create in great quantities and it is best to make arrangements to visit him so that an order can be placed. He will show his current creations as well as photographs of his work. One can ask for any type of animal. It takes some time to make them however, but they can be shipped inexpensively to the United States. After business has been concluded Señor Jimenez usually embraces his clients and gives them his blessing. Arrangements can be made to meet Señor Jimenez through Ms. Linda Anders who can be reached by writing to her at esq. Emilio Carranza Y Piños 221, Colonia Reforma, Oaxaca, Oaxaca, Mexico 68050.

More Sources

For those interested in purchasing *arte popular* the best sources are Victor's at Porfirio Diaz 111; FONART at M. Bravo 116 and Garcia Virgil; Yalalag at M. Acala 104; Artesanias Cocijo at Garcia Virgil 212; Casa Brena at Piño Suarez 58; and the State

Handicrafts Center on J. P. Garcia between Humbolt and Gomez Farias all of which are in Oaxaca City.

While busy with the excellent shopping Oaxaca has to offer, one should not overlook its two exceptional museums. The Regional Museum of Oaxaca and the Rufino Tamayo Museum of Pre-Hispanic Art are both intriguing enough, and small enough, to please even those who are not museum aficionados.

A Museum for Those who Hate Museums

The Regional Museum of Oaxaca is conveniently located next to Santo Domingo Church which is on the corner of Cinco de Mayo and Constitucion. The museum (a former convent) contains many exceptional pre-Hispanic works but is most famous for the treasure of gold artifacts found in Tomb Seven at the ruins of Monte Alban which are just outside of Oaxaca City.

Most scholars believe that the tomb, like the rest of the structures at Monte Alban, was constructed by the Zapotecs but was later taken over by the Mixtecs. A warrior people, the Mixtecs persistently harassed the Zapotecs but never conquered them. For some unknown reason the Zapotecs abandoned their capital, Monte Alban, and long after it had been deserted the Mixtecs took over the site and used Zapotec tombs for the burial of their own nobles. The cache found in Tomb Seven is the most extensive found in any of these tombs to date. Over 500 artifacts were discovered from which much new information was learned about the Mixtecs.

The Golden Treasure

One gallery of the Regional Museum of Oaxaca is devoted solely to the contents of Tomb Seven. Although the Mixtecs worked with many materials, the most fascinating pieces are those worked in gold. There is no question that the earrings, necklaces, pectorals, bracelets, as well as a crown, are supreme examples of the Mixtec goldsmiths' art. Some of the earrings are cast in the form of human faces and are exquisitely detailed. Necklaces consist of gold beads of varying sizes and shapes. Many contain only one strand of beads while others are made up of several strands. There are even those which incorporate as many as fifteen strands of gold beads. Other types of necklaces consist mainly of turquoise pieces interspersed with a few gold beads.

Masterpieces in Jade and Obsidian

There are also many other examples of Mixtec artistry exhibited in this gallery. Some of the most interesting are the carvings in jade and obsidian. The Mixtecs were also expert at minute carving and this can be clearly seen in their accurate and detailed carvings in bone.

Other masterpieces of Mixtec carving are a beautiful goblet carved from a solid piece of rock crystal and a goblet and pot carved from alabaster. The goblet, which has a tan coloration is intricately carved at its base. On the other hand, the white alabaster pot contains no ornamentation but intrigues because it seems to glow with an inner light.

A Human Skull

The most bizarre piece in the collection is the remnant of a human skull which is inlaid with turquoise. Although it would be difficult to term this work beautiful, it is powerful and it is not easily forgotten.

The artifacts from Tomb Seven are well displayed but they are difficult to photograph. Glass cases in this gallery often face each other and it is impossible not to get unwanted reflections in such a situation.

Other artifacts from Monte Alban and from other nearby archaeological sites are exhibited in other galleries. There is also an excellent site plan of Monte Alban as well as an aerial photograph of this site.

The Regional Museum of Oaxaca also has a section devoted to the various Indian cultures of the area as well as a section housing religious art relating to the history of the convent before it was converted into the museum. Both sections are worth some time.

Hints of a Colonial Past

Around the balcony of the convent's atrium one can also see the art of two distinct cultures. Large pre-Hispanic stone carvings have been placed around this balcony and they make an interesting contrast to the Colonial art in this area. On the columns of the balcony are paintings of saints done during the Colonial era. Also, remains of religious frescoes, created during the same period, adorn the upper walls of the atrium. These wall paintings are similar to those which remain at the Hotel El Presidente and reflect not only Mexico's colonial heritage but the history of this building as well.

Crash Course in Ancient Cultures

Oaxaca's other major museum, the Rufino Tamayo Museum of Pre-Hispanic Art, located at Avenida Morelos 503, is also housed in a restored colonial building. The museum, which is located only a few blocks from the Basilica de La Soledad, consists of five rooms which are situated around a tranquil central courtyard. The Tamayo Museum exhibits works from some of ancient Mexico's major cultures.

We See Ourselves

The Olmec pieces in this collection are interesting because it is quite easy to see the familiar in them. A helmeted Olmec figure, for example, sits with mouth open as if casually speaking. One arm rests upon a raised knee and in his hands he holds a club of bone or ivory which bears a carved design. Nearby, two Olmec female figures sit with hand on hip as if deep in conversation. Three other naked females lie on their stomach, their chins resting on their hands. They could be any group of women, of any time or place, sunning themselves. In these works we recognize ourselves and we are drawn to them.

In another gallery there is a figure from Jalisco which is on Mexico's Pacific Coast. In one hand this small figure holds up a large ball which looks very much like a modern basketball. It is yet another indication of the importance of the ritual ballgame in ancient Mexico.

Equally intriguing is a large stone slab which was carved on one side in Teotihuacan. The other side of the stone was carved by the Aztecs some seven hundred years later.

Skinned Victims

The museum also contains an interesting, large clay figure representing a priest wearing a mask of Xipe Totec, god of spring and of fertility. As part of the rites of this god, victims were skinned and Xipe Totec's priests then wore the skin which symbolized the new covering the earth takes on each year.

Besides numerous small figures representing ancient Mexico's ritual ballgame, the Tamayo Museum also exhibits a large number of *hachas* carved in the form of animals. Though it is known that these stone implements were used in the game, their exact use is unclear. It is thought that players used the *hachas* to hit the ball with greater force.

The museum is also noted for two intricately carved Maya stelae from Campeche. As they are displayed here, visitors are afforded an excellent opportunity for a detailed inspection of the artistry involved in creating them.

Master and Captives

Another beautiful Maya work is exhibited in the courtyard area of the museum and should not be overlooked. It is a stone panel representing a Maya overlord or *jefe* seated upon two captives. The panel is finely carved and the postures of the figures are typically Mayan.

Not Overwhelming

All of the works in the Rufino Tamayo Museum are exhibited as art and not as historical curiosities. Although the collection is extensive, it is not overwhelming and one could not ask for a more pleasant setting in which to experience art.

Endless Fascination

Oaxaca's two museums, its shops, nearby villages, Indian markets, colonial buildings and its proximity to major archaeological sites make it an extremely interesting area to visit. Because Oaxaca combines Indian, Colonial and modern cultures, it is always fascinating.

Chapter 7

MONTE ALBAN

Sky City of Gods and Priests

The spectacular archaeological site of Monte Alban, which is open from 8 a.m. to 6 p.m. daily, is only five miles from the city of Oaxaca and can be easily reached by bus, rental car or taxi. However, rental cars are often hard to obtain in Oaxaca and it may be more feasible to take a bus or to hire a car with driver. Usually, a car with driver is less expensive than a rental car and since drivers are from the area they are familiar with local roads.

False Impression

Since the structures at Monte Alban are no longer highly ornamented, one's first impression is that all the buildings look alike. Upon closer inspection it is obvious that, though the structures are similar, each is distinctive. In ancient times, however, the buildings were covered with a hard substance which was painted in bright colors. Buildings were also covered with figures and stylized motifs which, except in a few instances, have not survived the centuries.

City in the Sky

This ancient city rests upon a man-made plateau. To build their capital, the Zapotecs leveled the top of a mountain, doing so without the aid of the wheel or beasts of burden.

Monte Alban was built in phases over a period of centuries with many structures being built upon existing ones. For the Zapotecs, Monte Alban was a city of the gods. Because of the altitude of its location the city even gives a sense of the mystical to modern day visitors. This was a place for priests whose needs were met by the populace. There is no water source at Monte Alban and no crops were grown here. All supplies had to be carried up from the valley 1200 feet below.

Exceptional Achievements

The Zapotecs were skilled engineers and architects. They also developed a system of numbers, an accurate calendar, hiero-

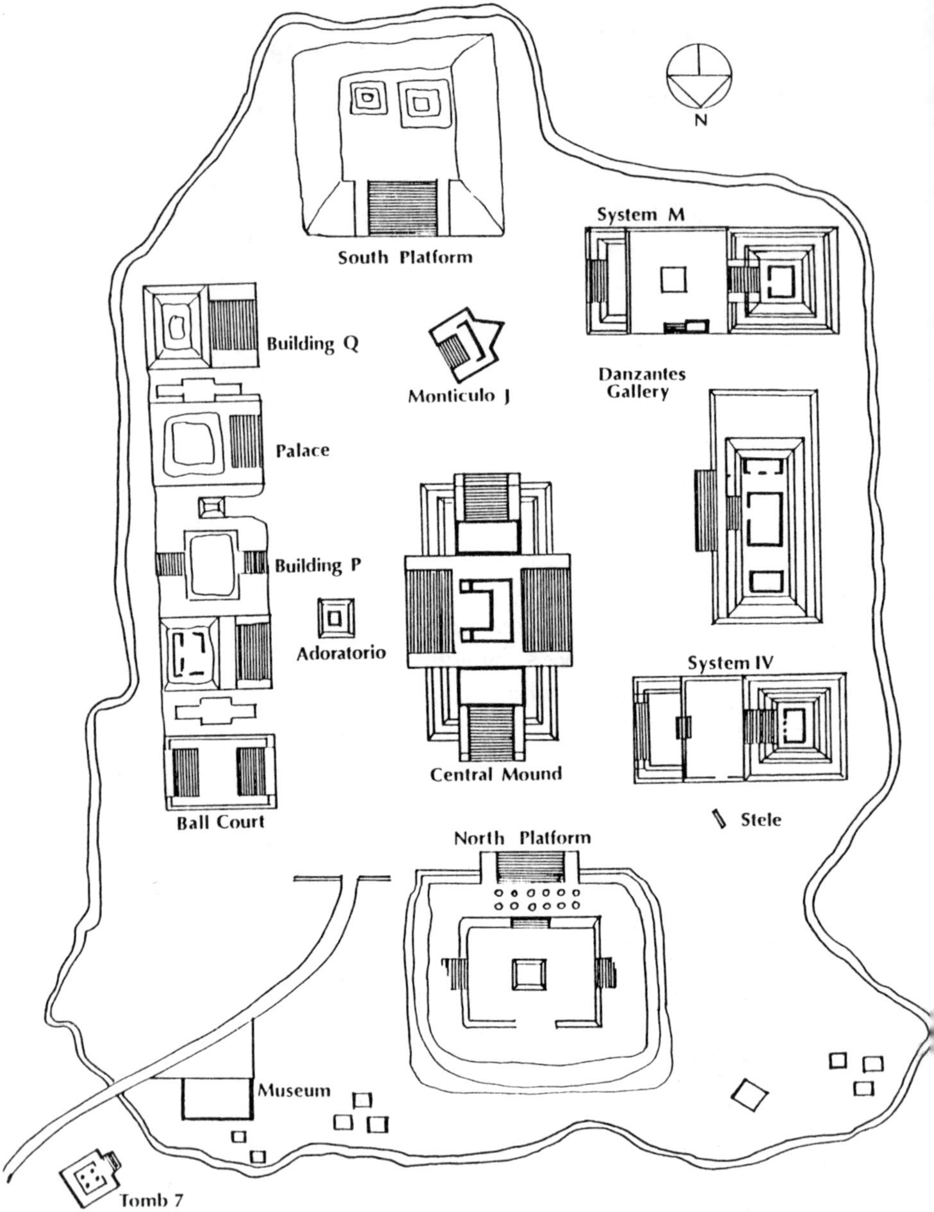
N
South Platform
System M
Building Q
Monticulo J
Danzantes
Gallery
Palace
Building P
Adoratorio
System IV
Central Mound
Ball Court
Stele
North Platform
Museum
Tomb 7

MONTE ALBAN

glyphic writing, practiced herbal medicine and were astute astronomical observers. Their artistic sense was also highly developed and they created many highly detailed works. With the exception of the stone carvings at Monte Alban, most Zapotec figures are characterized by one or more of the following details: elaborate headdresses, oversized ear ornaments and large protruding teeth.

The mountaintop acropolis of Monte Alban is a testament to the skill and artistry of the Zapotecs. There is much to see at this site and sufficient time should be allotted to enjoy the splendor of Monte Alban at a leisurely pace. Since the sun's rays are more intense at this altitude a sun lotion is recommended as is a hat.

Easiest Way to Visit Site

Unlike most ancient sites in Mexico, the structures at Monte Alban have not been given romantic or exotic names. Most structures at the site are simply designated by a letter. Unfortunately, this system can make it difficult, but not impossible, to figure out what one is looking at. The central area of Monte Alban contains thirteen structures which form a huge rectangle with three structures in the center. However, it is not necessary to climb all of them.

The first structure one comes upon at Monte Alban is the ball court. Common throughout ancient Mexico, the ballgame was of ritual importance. Unlike its modern counterparts, the game was not played simply for sport and the stakes were much higher. Although much is not known about this ancient sport, it is believed that the losing team was sacrificed. The ball court at Monte Alban has been restored but, like the other structures, it lacks the brightly colored stucco with which it was covered in ancient times.

From this area it is best to proceed in a more or less clockwise direction around the rest of the site. Doing so, the next structures one comes upon are the Eastside Platform, followed by Building P, the Palace and Building Q. Of this group, the Palace is the most interesting and is worth climbing for the views it affords of the Central Mound.

Excellent Vantage Point for Photographs

The Central Mound is situated in the center of Monte Alban and consists of a series of interconnecting buildings, designated buildings G, H and I. The city's main altar was located in this area. The Central Mound is an interesting section of the site to explore and affords excellent vantage points from which to photograph many of the other structures at Monte Alban.

Between the Palace, Building P and the Central Mound is a sunken area known as the Adoratorio. It was here that a mask of the Zapotec bat god was uncovered. This magnificent work in jade and shell was, unfortunately, stolen in 1985 from the National Museum of Anthropology in Mexico City.

At the southern end of the Central Mound stands Monticulo J, one of the most interesting structures at Monte Alban. Also known as the Observatory, Monticulo J contains interesting carvings of figures which have been incorporated into the building. A tunnel, which is open at its top, transverses this structure and contains interesting carved hieroglyphs.

Great View of a Female Nude

Just past Monticulo J, at the extreme southern end of Monte Alban's Great Plaza, is the South Platform. It is the largest structure at Monte Alban but little reconstruction has been done on it. The base of this structure contains a number of large stone blocks which bear carved glyphs and figures. Some are copies, however, since some of the originals were moved to Mexico City. One of the most interesting figures in this area is a carving of a reclining nude female who has one arm extended above her head. The figure seems to be swimming which is startling because Monte Alban is so arid. Other interesting carved blocks can also be seen lying about between Monticulo J and the South Platform.

The climb to the top of the South Platform is tiring but worth the effort. Because the top of this platform is high above the Great Plaza, it affords an excellent overview of the entire site.

System M, consisting of two buildings and a court, stands at the southwest corner of the Great Plaza. This structure is worth some exploration and from its summit one is afforded a panorama of the valley 1200 feet below.

Dancers in Stone?

At this end of the plaza is the Danzantes Gallery, containing the most famous artifacts at Monte Alban. These human figures carved on large stone slabs are located between System M and a structure known as the Danzantes Building. These figures have given rise to much speculation. Because most seem to be in motion, they were thought to be dancers, hence the Spanish appellation *danzantes*. These figures date from the earliest period of occupation at Monte Alban. The carvings are all of males. Some are young, some old. Some of the figures portray hunchbacks or other deformities. Also, many of the figures bear strong negroid features which possibly indicate contact with the Olmec civilization far to the south. Although the figures are in various postures, they do not represent dancers. One theory is that the figures are anatomical drawings and represent a medical book in stone. It is more likely, however, that the figures represent the mutilated bodies of conquered rulers who were sacrificed to Zapotec gods.

Flowing Genitals

The postures of the figures and their nudity are taken as evidence that these figures represent captives. One of the most curious aspects of these figures is that many of them contain unusual designs carved in the area of the genitals. Flowing from the genitals are designs which have been interpreted as liquid, scrolls or flowers. The meaning of these representations has, thus far, eluded scholars.

Photographers Take Note

The best time to photograph the Danzantes is during the morning since, at this time of day, the figures stand out most clearly.

Getting Inside

Beyond the Danzantes Gallery are the Danzantes Building and System IV, which is almost identical to System M. Both structures offer exceptional views of the valley below Monte Alban as well as of the west side of the Central Mound. In modern times tunnels were excavated through these structures allowing visitors to view the earlier buildings which lie within. A small flashlight is most helpful since sections of these tunnels are not well lighted.

Leaving the Tourist Trail

Before leaving the central area of Monte Alban, some time should be spent exploring the area of the North Platform. At this point one has made a complete circle of the site. Like the other structures at Monte Alban, the North Platform has a great stairway. Above this stairway are the remains of twelve columns and a sunken court at the center of which is an altar. This altar may have been of greater importance than the one uncovered at the Central Mound.

Little excavation has been done in the area of the North Platform and, for those with a strong interest in archaeology, it is an interesting section in which to wander. The possibility of seeing what few people have seen is a strong incentive for some to investigate this area of Monte Alban.

Beyond the North Platform are mounds which have not been excavated. Climbing these mounds provides a view of the Monte Alban Museum, the temple above Tomb Seven and Oaxaca City below, in the valley. Sunset is a particularly beautiful time to visit this area because the city of Oaxaca appears to shimmer in the distance.

More Danzantes and a Tomb

Before leaving Monte Alban, it would be a good idea to visit the small museum which houses artifacts found at the site. Also, some of the Danzantes have been moved to the museum in an effort to preserve them.

Across the road from the museum and parking area is a small temple under which is Tomb Seven. The tomb is often locked and, except for those with a serious interest in archaeology, visiting the area is not recommended. It is unfortunate that this tomb cannot be visited for it was here that the Mixtec artifacts, exhibited at the Regional Museum of Oaxaca, were found.

Descendants Abound

Anyone visiting the Oaxaca area should not miss visiting Monte Alban. After visiting this site, it is hard not to be in awe of the achievements of these ancient Americans. Although the Zapotecs and Mixtecs who toiled at Monte Alban have long passed from this earth, their works endure and their descendants live in the outlying villages of Oaxaca State and can be seen at the Indian Market.

Chapter 8

MITLA, YAGUL, LAMBITYECO and DAINZU

Designs for Eternity Most Never See

Besides the major ruins of Monte Alban, Oaxaca State contains other archaeological sites which, though smaller in scale, are extremely interesting. Conveniently located near Oaxaca City, Mitla, Yagul, Lambityeco and Dainzu can easily be visited in a single day trip by car. Of these four sites, Mitla (open 9 a.m.-5 p.m. daily) is the farthest from Oaxaca City and is the most important archaeological site in the area after Monte Alban. It is best to visit Mitla first and then visit Yagul, Lambityeco and Dainzu as one heads back to Oaxaca City.

Builders Subject of Controversy

There is some controversy as to whether Mitla was constructed by the Zapotecs or by the Mixtecs but it is generally accepted that the Mixtecs created the fretwork designs which adorn the buildings and for which Mitla is justly famous.

Unrivaled Jewelers

The Mixtecs were an aggressive, warrior people. Yet, despite their preoccupation with war, they created works of great artistic refinement and beauty. The skill of their goldsmiths is unrivaled. The art of human adornment was raised to a high level by the Mixtecs and, besides gold, masterworks were created in turquoise, jade and shell.

Books on Skin

Another aspect of the Mixtec cultural legacy is the codices they created. These deer skin books, which contain pictures and glyphs, are vibrant with color and are rich in visual detail. Though not fully understood, the codices can be appreciated for their beauty and visual power.

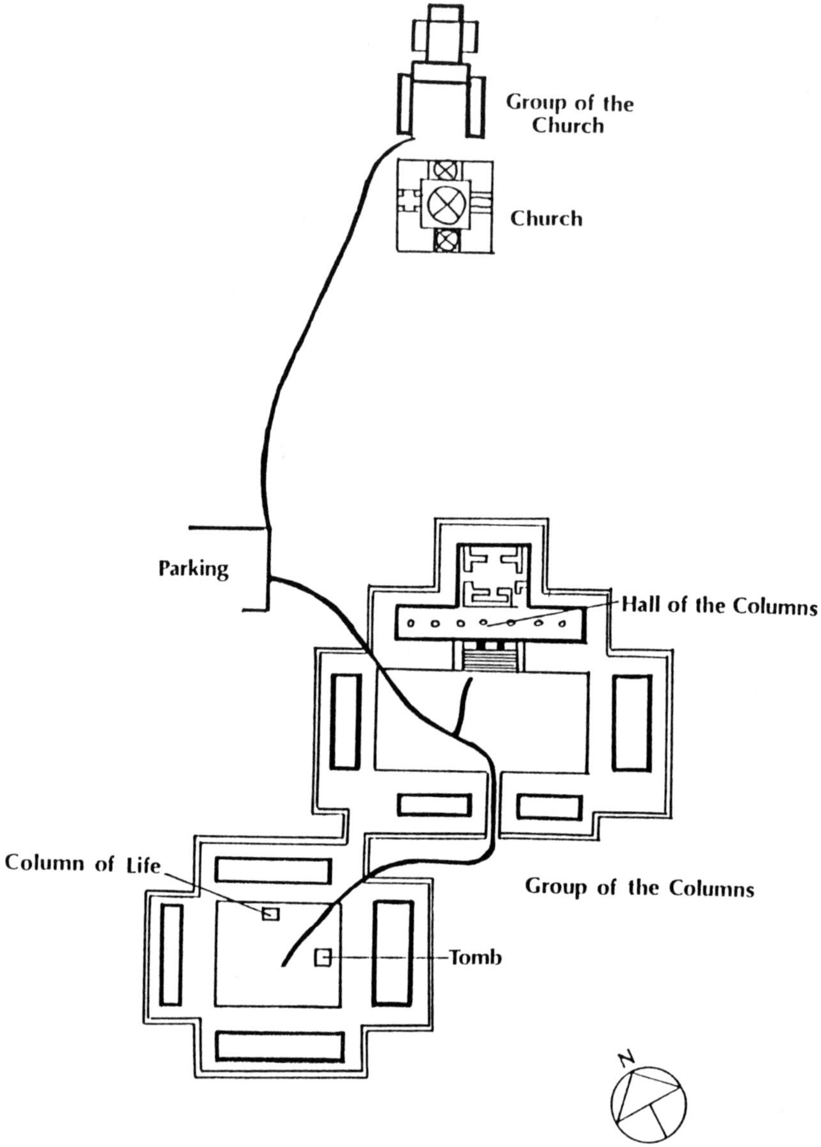
Group of the
Church
Church
Parking
Hall of the Columns
Column of Life
Group of the Columns
Tomb
N

MITLA

Unique Designs

At Mitla, the Mixtec art of architectural embellishment can be seen. Visitors to the site often walk about and wonder aloud at the intricacy of the cut stone fretwork. There are a variety of designs which were used by the Mixtecs at Mitla. Because the cut stone stands out from the buildings, there is a constant play of light and shadow upon them causing them to appear ever changing. The designs seem to undulate as they swirl and twist across the buildings and they are an endless source of wonderment and fascination. These fretwork designs are what is most impressive about Mitla.

In ancient times, Mitla encompassed a much larger area than can be seen today. Of what remains, only a few sections are of interest to most visitors. These are the Group of the Columns, the tomb containing the Column of Life and the Group of the Church.

Area for Color Photography

The Group of the Columns consists of buildings constructed around two large courtyards. The first court contains numerous examples of Mixtec fretwork designs and is noteworthy for the Hall of Columns. This hall contains the remains of six huge columns and is at the north end of the first courtyard. The facade of this hall contains remnants of the paint with which it was covered in ancient times which makes it an excellent area for color photography. Adjoining this hall are a number of small rooms containing fine examples of Mixtec fretwork designs and are well worth exploring.

How Long Will You Live?

The second court of the Group of the Columns, though not as interesting as the first, contains tombs which visitors might want to investigate. The tombs are small, do not contain much to see and they can be rather hot and humid. Oddly enough, however, being underground in the smallness of the tombs, one feels eerily close to the ancients. The most interesting of these tombs is the one containing the Column of Life. According to local custom, it is possible to determine the length of one's life by putting one's arms around the column. The greater the distance between one's hands, the longer one will live. Hopefully, one's hands will not meet.

Fragments of Fabulous Frescoes

The other major area to be seen at Mitla is the Group of the Church which consists of a Catholic Church and a series of Mixtec rooms behind it. The church was constructed from the stones of Mitla's buildings and its exterior is of more interest than its interior. The remains of Mixtec rooms are interesting in terms of construction and, especially, for the remnants of frescoes in this area. If one looks carefully, it is possible to find quite a number of these beautiful fragments which give some idea of how these rooms were decorated when used by the Mixtecs.

Tips on Mitla's Market

Besides the ruins, Mitla has a tourist market, shops and a small museum. The market is just outside the ruins and the vendors tend to be more aggressive than in other areas. Prices are generally high and rugs sold as made of pure wool often are not. Rugs are best purchased in Teotitlan del Valle. Time would be better spent browsing shops located on the street leading up to the ruins from the highway.

An Often Overlooked Museum

Located in the town of Mitla is a small museum built around a courtyard. This museum, known as the Museum of Zapotec Art as well as the Mitla Museum and the Frissell Museum, contains quite a number of artifacts found at Mitla and other nearby sites. The larger pieces are exhibited in the courtyard area and the caretaker will gladly open a small, locked room so the smaller pieces can be viewed. This room contains numerous figures of varying sizes, most of which are figures of Cocijo, the Zapotec rain god.

Small and Interesting

After visiting Mitla, brief stops can be made at Yagul, Lambityeco and Dainzu as one returns to Oaxaca City. Although these sites are not extensive, each is interesting in its own way.

Giant Carving Most Never Notice

Yagul is approximately seven miles from Mitla and twenty miles from Oaxaca City. Just after turning off the main highway as one is heading toward Yagul, there is a large petroglyph carved into a cliff some distance to the right. This carving can be seen with the unaided eye but a telephoto lens offers the best view.

Upon entering Yagul, one is immediately struck by the fact that the fretwork designs of the buildings bear a striking similarity to those of Mitla.

Yagul was inhabited by the Mixtecs and the Zapotecs at various times and the influences of these cultures is evident, especially if one has visited Monte Alban and Mitla.

How to Get Into a Tomb

The main area of Yagul is known as the Acropolis and consists of a number of buildings and their courtyards. This section also contains an unusually large and beautifully restored ball court as well as some tombs. The most interesting of these burial chambers is Tomb Thirty. The entrance of this tomb is decorated with fretwork designs and carved stone heads. In general, the tombs are kept locked but the caretaker will usually open them for visitors. It is customary to give the caretaker a small tip for doing so. Before entering the tombs one should be aware that the tombs are hot and, because their ceilings are so low, it is necessary to move about in a squatting position.

Great Panoramas

For overall views of the site, as well as of the surrounding area, it is necessary to follow a small path to the highest section of Yagul known as the Great Fortress. This is an excellent area for photography.

Ancient Faces Unearthed

Two miles closer to Oaxaca City is the much smaller site of Lambityeco. Like other sites in this area, in ancient times, Lambityeco covered a much larger area. For most visitors, the cut stone friezes depicting an elderly couple and the stucco heads on the tombs are what is of interest. One of the tombs bears stucco heads of another elderly man and woman. Another tomb is decorated with two stucco heads of the god Cocijo who is represented with a huge headdress and oversized ear ornaments. The stucco heads of this god are magnificent.

Unfortunately, the friezes and the stucco heads are behind locked fences and are shielded from the sun by metal awnings.

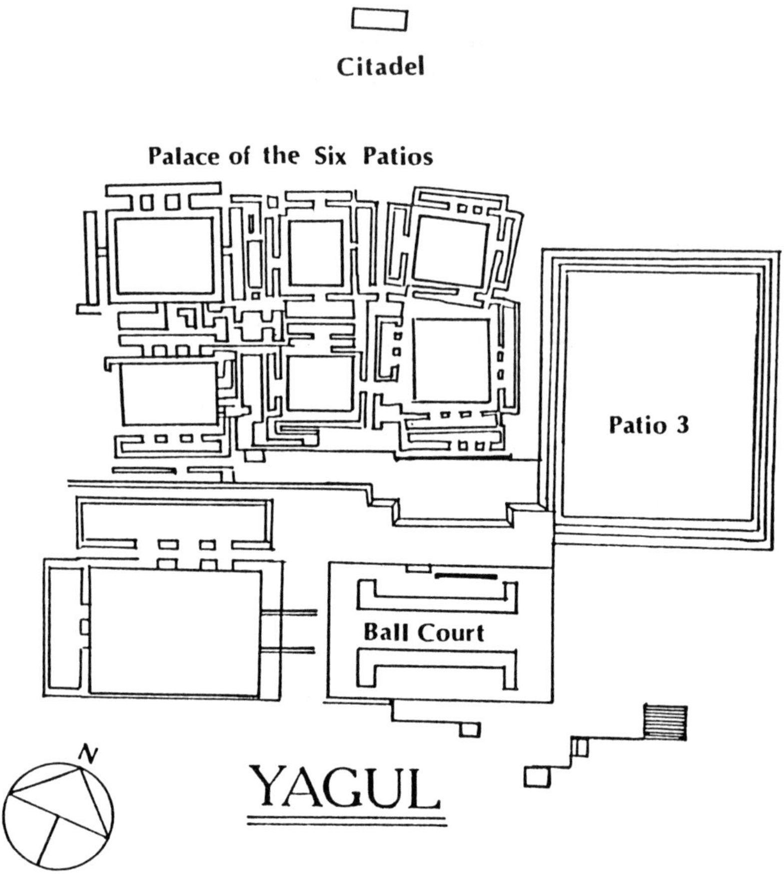

There is a caretaker at Lambityeco who might be persuaded to open the locked gates of these areas so one can get a better view and better photographs. If this cannot be arranged, a telephoto lens will solve the problem.

Ball Players and a Jaguar Tomb

Five miles from Lambityeco is the Zapotec site of Dainzu. This site has three main points to recommend, at least, a brief visit: carved slabs, a carved tomb entrance and a partially restored ball court.

There are fifty carved stone slabs at Dainzu and they are similar in style to the Danzantes of Monte Alban. The majority of the slabs represent human figures thought to be ball players. Unfortunately, most of the figures are not as well preserved as those at Monte Alban and they do not photograph as well.

More easily photographed is a tomb entrance carved in the form of a jaguar. This jaguar is made up of three pieces. The legs are carved on two vertical side posts and the shoulders and head are represented on the crossbeam. For photographic purposes the jaguar entrance receives the best light from late morning through early afternoon.

Similar to the ball court at Yagul, the one at Dainzu is of interest because only half of it has been restored. The contrast between the restored section and the pile of rubble which is the unrestored section is thought provoking. It gives some idea of the work which was involved in restoring Mexico's archaeological wonders. It also gives a clear idea of the state into which most of these wonders had fallen.

From Dainzu it is only a short thirteen miles back to Oaxaca City. After having visited Mitla, Yagul, Lambityeco, and Dainzu one cannot but admire the people who created them.

DAINZU

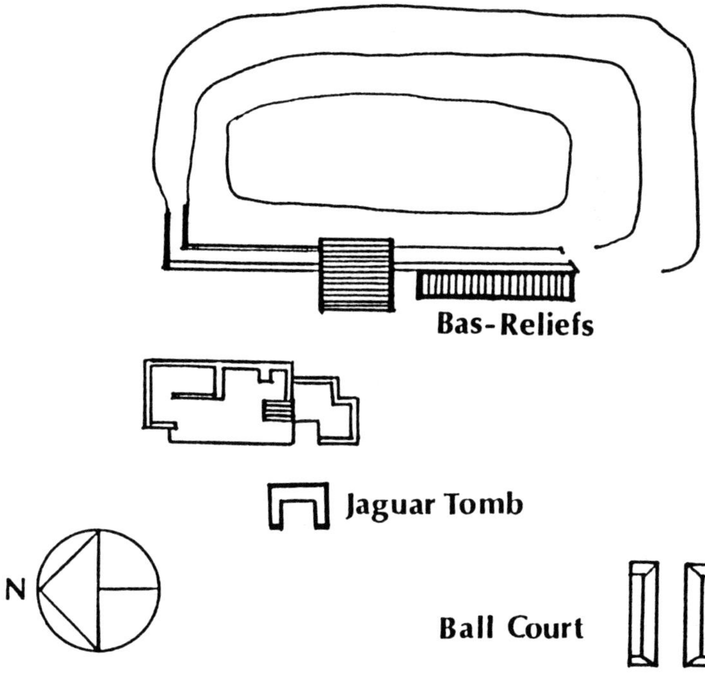

CHAPTER 9
Villahermosa
Colossal Heads

Most travel guides malign Villahermosa as a place that should be either passed through as quickly as possible or as one that should be avoided altogether. Although not nearly as charming as many other Mexican cities, Villahermosa does have a number of things to recommend it to the traveler. Unfortunately, most travelers who come to this city fly in on their way to Palenque and usually drive directly from the airport to these ruins, thereby missing what Villahermosa has to offer.

Best and most Convenient Hotel

The old section of the city is not without its charm and it is possible to take dinner cruises on the Grijalva River which winds its way past Villahermosa. The selection of hotels in Villahermosa is, admittedly, limited. By far, the best is the Hyatt Villahermosa. Although this large hotel lacks charm, it is clean, well run and has most of the amenities one could desire. The Hyatt is also within easy walking distance of La Venta Park. This archaeological park and the CICOM Museum are the main reasons for visiting this city. Each is spectacular, in its own way, and neither should be missed.

World's most Unusual Park

La Venta Park is unique. Displayed within a tropical setting are massive archaeological finds. The huge stone carvings were moved from the original La Venta site and most were brought to this specially designed park in Villahermosa which is open daily from 8:30 a.m. to 5 p.m. The park is located near the Circuito del Golfo near the Paseo Tabasco. Each piece was placed exactly as it was found at the original site. Seeing these monumental works in this natural setting makes the Olmecs, who created them, seem less obscure and more human.

Mother Culture of the Americas

Many scholars believe that the Olmec civilization was the mother culture of ancient Meso-America. The influence of these ancient people extended over the area that is today Mexico and Central America. In comparison to other ancient peoples, little is known with certainty about the Olmecs. Their origins are unclear as is their ultimate fate. Even their appearance is a subject of conjecture since the features of their monumental works are in sharp contrast to those of their smaller creations.

Although the Olmecs also created small works, it is usually their monumental stone creations which first capture the imagination and seductively lure one into a further investigation of this mysterious culture. Amid the outdoor setting of La Venta Park the full power of these massive sculptures can be felt in a way that is somehow lost when such works are contained within the walls of a conventional museum. As with all art, knowledge adds a certain degree of appreciation but one can simply respond to these works on an intuitive level. After seeing them, however, it is hard to resist the desire to know more about these people who created on such a grand scale.

When to Visit and What to Bring

An early morning visit to La Venta Park is suggested since Villahermosa is often hot and humid and becomes more so as the day progresses. Because of this climate, insect repellent is essential for warding off mosquitoes. Bearing these recommendations in mind, one can spend a few pleasant hours in this very special place. Amid lush foliage one can enjoy monumental works of art while surrounded by the sounds of birds and the sight of fluttering butterflies.

Exotic Creatures Abound

Another pleasure of this unusual park is its small collection of animals which were important to Olmec culture. Much to the surprise and delight of visitors, some of these creatures wander freely and tourists are often greeted at the entrance by a friendly coatimundi. Although they appear to be quite tame, one should not attempt to pet any of the free-roaming monkeys or coatimundis. As with any animal, however tame, there is always the possibility that they will bite strangers. These animals are also quite willing, even anxious, to accept treats. The temptation to feed them should be resisted. Most visitors give pieces of candy and this is not a healthy practice.

Hypnotic, Floating Eyes

Throughout the park, in various enclosures, one can also see an ocelot, deer and crocodiles. The jaguar, because of its significance in Olmec art, is the most important animal in the collection and should not be missed. Through their art, we know that the Olmecs were seemingly obsessed with the concept of a man-jaguar. Although caged, the jaguar in La Venta Park is nonetheless frightening. One can appreciate the awe and reverence the Olmecs felt for this cat. This is especially evident when the light causes the cat's eyes to take on an unearthly, green glow and to appear to float beyond its head. When this occurs the eyes have a frighteningly hypnotic quality.

Although the animals of La Venta Park are fascinating, it is the man-made works that are of primary interest. Since there is no longer much to see at the original La Venta site, a small reproduction, just beyond the entrance to the park, gives the visitor a good indication of what it looked like. From this point on, one has only to follow the well marked path which runs through the park. All of the artifacts in La Venta Park are of interest but some are more impressive than others.

Ferocity in Stone

Monument One, for example, has been termed a stone altar but may have served some other purpose. This huge piece represents the snarling face of some animal, most probably a jaguar. Even though a good portion of the features are missing, it does evoke a sense of animal ferocity.

Ancient Sun Worshipper?

Of a more tranquil tone, Monument Two is a stone figure with its arms behind its upturned head, seemingly basking in the sun. Except for the arms, the body is a simple gray column. However, the face is highly detailed and interesting. Two tone in color, the area below the nose is off-white while the area above is the same natural gray stone as the rest of the figure.

A much larger piece, Monument Six is a huge rectangle often

referred to as an altar. Although there are bas-reliefs at each end, it is the figure in the niche on the front which is most arresting. Seated with legs crossed and leaning forward, the figure seems ready to emerge from the rock. The figure's right hand clutches an object while the left hand clutches the right ankle. As adornment, the figure is wearing broad bracelets, a pectoral, collar and headdress.

On a smaller scale, Monument Nine is also a cross-legged figure but the fists rest on the knees. The figure is typical of smaller Olmec human representations because of the severe frown on the face and because of its flabby, childlike body.

Heads Without Bodies

One of the main reasons people visit La Venta Park is to see the huge, stone heads created by the Olmecs. Three of them (Monuments Eleven, Twenty-Five and Twenty-Seven) are displayed within this park. No one knows why the Olmecs created these heads weighing approximately twenty tons. They were never intended to have bodies and, after being created, were ritually buried by the Olmecs. Although similar in expression, no two are exactly alike and each wears a distinctive helmet. The significance of these helmets has given rise to a number of theories. Perhaps they were worn by warriors or signified kingship. Since the Olmecs, like other ancient Americans, may have played a ritual ballgame, the helmets may possibly represent those worn by ballplayers. These massive, stone heads have given rise to other theories as well.

Visits from Ancient Africa?

For example, many people have felt that the faces of these sculptures have Negroid features. This has been the basis for much speculation about contact between the Olmecs and ancient African peoples. However, there is no evidence to support this theory and the features of the stone sculptures do resemble those of the modern inhabitants of the area.

Though not of monumental size, Monument Twenty is nonetheless interesting. It is a small, seated figure wearing a helmet-like headdress and holding out what may be an offering plate. The legs of the figure are extremely short and stump-like. The head of this figure makes an interesting contrast to the monumental heads.

Messages from the Olmec Past

Because of its hieroglyphs, Monument Twenty-Two is of great interest. Olmec writing is as yet undeciphered but a number of possible interpretations have been put forth for those on this work. This rounded stone slab portrays, in profile, the complete figure of a bearded male. The figure is wearing a headdress, about his waist is a broad sash and in his left hand he carries what may be a banner or a weapon. In front of the figure are three glyphs which may signify his name and rank. Behind the figure is a footprint which probably signifies travel.

Looking very much like a hut made out of green stone poles, monument Twenty-four was, in fact, a burial site. It is quite beautiful in its simplicity and is one of the many unusual sights in this park.

Contact with Ancient Orient?

Monument Twenty-Nine is larger but strikingly similar to Monument Six. The figure in the niche of Monument Twenty-Nine holds out what is thought to be a were-jaguar. As with Monument Six, both ends of this colossal stone rectangle bear bas-reliefs. The details of these reliefs are exquisite. The eyes of these figures and the shape of their heads are in direct contrast to those of the figure in the niche as well as to the features of the monumental heads. These features have given rise to speculation about contact with the ancient Orient. Once again, the visitor is left wondering about the true appearance of these ancient people. Perhaps it is the very scarcity of knowledge about the Olmecs which makes them so maddeningly fascinating and exotic.

Unexplained Feats

After visiting La Venta Park one is in awe of the modern engineering feat of transporting the huge artifacts to Villahermosa from their original site eighty miles away. Imagine what engineering skills the Olmecs possessed. Without the use of the wheel, they moved the massive stones, weighing tons, sixty miles to the original La Venta site!

Beauty Seen by Too Few

Seeing only the monumental works the Olmecs created would

National Museum of Anthropology
Mexico City

1. Pacal's jade death mask from Palenque

2. Detail of column from Xochicalco ruins

3. Detail of Maya stele from Yachilan

4. Aztec calendar stone in Aztec Hall

5. Reproduction: "Paradise of Tlaloc" Teotihuacan fresco

6. *Remains of monumental bas-relief*

7. *Stone carving of Tlaltecuhtli, god of earth*

Templo Mayor Museum
Mexico City

8. *Stone statues*

9. *Monumental carved stone shell*

10. *Gold jewelry, Gallery 8*

11   12.

11. Squatting figure of Tlaloc, alabaster—Gallery 5

12. Architectural embellishment in form of stylized snail

Templo Mayor Museum
Mexico City

13. Stone of Coyolxauhqui viewed from Gallery 4

14. Aztec flint ceremonial blades with human faces

15. Polychromed effigy vessel of Tlaloc—Gallery 5

Templo Mayor Museum
Mexico City

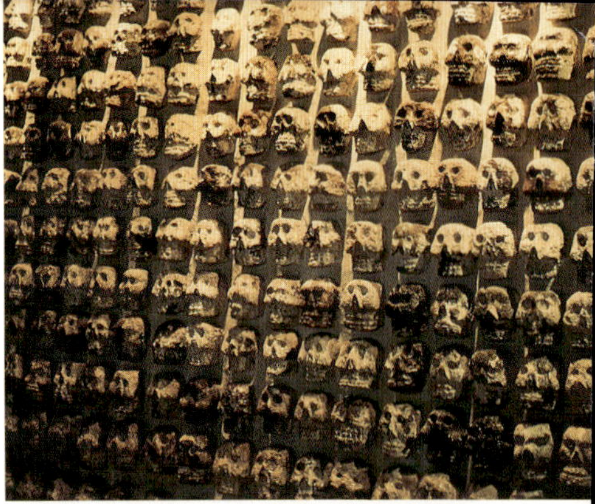

16. Portion of Tzompantli (skull rack)

17. Original figure found in Temple of Huitzilopochtli

18. Monumental brazier—Gallery 3

19. Teotihuacan-style jade mask—Gallery 3

20. Monumental stone eagle—Gallery I

National Palace—Mexico City
Murals by Diego Rivera

21. *Courtyard of the National Palace*

22. *Diego Rivera mural in the courtyard*

23. *Detail: "The Great City of Tenochtitlan"*

24. *Detail: "The Great City of Tenochtitlan"*

25. *Detail: "The Totonac Civilization"*

26. Detail of the Palace of Quetzalpapalotl at Teotithuacan

27. Monumental plumed serpent head Temple of Quetzalcoatl at Teotithuacan

28. Row of stone and mortar serpents at Tenayuca

28.

29. Pyramid of Santa Cecelia Acatitlan

30. Traditional Mexican kitchen at Sant Cecelia Acatitlan Museum

31. Large stone and mortar coiled serpent at Tenayuca

32. Tenayuca pyramid—the outskirts of Mexico City

33. Pyramid of the Atlantes at Tula

34. Stucco reliefs, each side of Pyramid of the Atlantes at Tula

35. The Atlantes atop the Pyramid of the Atlantes at Tula

36. Building decorated with tiles in Puebla

37. Villas Arqueologicas Hotel in Tula

38. Stone Building restoration, west side of Great Pyramid (Cholula)

39. Overview of ruins and church atop the Great Pyramid (Cholula)

40. Colonial church atop Great Pyramid at Cholula

41. *Tajin Chico, Building D, El Tajin*

42. *Mixtec gold piece from Tomb 7, Monte Alban, in Oaxaca Museum*

43. *Platform, Building 5, and Pyramid of the Niches at El Tajin*

44. *Tajin Chico, Building C, El Tajin*

45. *Black pottery and Zapotec rug (Collection of Thayer Durell, Jr.)*

46. *Monticulo J at Monte Alban*

48. *System M and Danzantes Gallery at Monte Alban*

47. *System IV at Monte Alban*

49. *Danzantes at Monte Alban*

50. *A Danzante at Monte Alban*

51. *Courtyard, Hall of the Columns at Mitla*

52. *Group of the Columns area at Mitla*

53. *Jaguar tomb at Dainzu*

54. *Ball court at Yagul*

55. *Detail of a tomb entrance at Yagul*

56. Incised Mayan vessel at CICOM Museum in Villahermosa

57. Mask of the god Cocijo at Lambityeco

58. Detail of Monument Twenty-Nine at La Venta Park, Villahermosa →

59. Monument Six in La Venta Park at Villahermosa

60. Monument Twenty-Nine at La Venta Park, Villahermosa

61.

62.

61. Temple of the Sun from Temple of the Cross at Palenque

62. Bas-relief, northeast court of Palace Complex at Palenque

63. Temple of Inscriptions from the Palace Tower at Palenque

64. Large stucco head, north facade of Palace at Palenque

65. Carnaval day parade at Merida

66. Pyramid of the Five Stories at Etzna

67. Palace of the Governor at Uxmal

68. Great Pyramid at Uxmal

69. The Palace at Kabah

70. The Codz-Poop at Kabah

71. The Palace at Sayil

72. Hook-nosed Chaac mask at Sayil

73. Doorway with Chaac masks at Xlapak

74.

74. Palace detail at Labna

75. Structure with Chaac mask at Mayapan

76. The Observatory at Mayapan

77. Broken Chac-mool at Chichen Itza

78. Detail: Temple of the Warriors at Chichen Itza

79. Temple of the Warriors at Chichen Itza

80. Tzompantli (skull rack) at Chichen Itza

81. Temple of the Descending God at Tulum

82. El Castillo at Tulum

give a distorted impression of their artistic achievements. Within the CICOM Museum one can view Olmec works created on a more human scale. Though smaller, these pieces are nonetheless masterfully executed.

Situated on the banks of the Grijalva River, the CICOM Museum is open from Tuesday to Sunday from 10 a.m. to 1 p.m. and then from 5 p.m. to 8 p.m. Within the museum are works created by the Olmecs, the Maya and other ancient Mexican cultures. The CICOM museum is part of a small complex containing a restaurant and shops and is a pleasant spot to pass a few hours.

Throughout the CICOM Museum smaller Olmec works are displayed to optimum advantage. The ground floor contains most of the larger Olmec and Maya pieces in the collection. Ample natural lighting is provided on this floor by oversized windows which face the river.

Human Monster

Each work exhibited throughout the museum holds its own fascination. However, on the ground level, most visitors are immediately intrigued by a large squatting figure. This large stone sculpture with its head thrust back seems to be snarling to the heavens. The large fangs of this human-like figure give it a stong feline quality. The Olmecs portrayed such features with great frequency in their art. These features, which are part human and part cat, support the belief that the concept of a were-jaguar played an important part in Olmec religion.

Enigmatic Smile

Also found on this level is an Olmec stone head. Though not of monumental size, the contrast between this work and those at La Venta Park is quite sharp. The Olmec head at the CICOM Museum is not only much smaller but the features are subtly different from those of the colossal heads. The smaller work does wear a helmet but, unlike the larger heads, also wears a somewhat enigmatic smile.

Ancient Eyeglasses?

A very curious piece is a stone figure wearing a strange helmet-like headdress and standing with arms folded. The most unusual aspect of this ancient figure is that it is wearing what appear to be goggles or eyeglasses! There may be a simple explanation for this but it is just such unexpected touches which have given rise to theories that the Olmecs, as well as other ancients, were visited by extraterrestrials.

Nude Torso

A few steps away is a seated nude torso. The head is missing as are the arms and little is left of the legs. Nonetheless, this Olmec stone sculpture is intriguing. Although little remains of this piece, it is somehow strangely reminiscent of ancient Greek and Roman works.

Palenque Previews

For those traveling on to Palenque, a stucco torso may also be of interest. This Mayan work is not only beautiful but can also serve as an introduction, in close-up, to the stucco reliefs found at the Palenque ruins.

Another Mayan work which should not be overlooked is a large rectangular stone slab. Around its edges are exquisitely carved Mayan glyphs. These beautiful examples of Maya picture writing make excellent choices for close-up photography.

Mayan hieroglyphs can also be seen on a large stela. Besides containing quite a number of glyphs, this large upright stone slab contains a beautiful bas-relief of a Maya personage wearing a large headdress. It is interesting to compare this stela to one nearby which contains eight large glyphs and a bas-relief of a cat.

Heart of the Collection

What many consider to be the heart of this collection can be seen in the mezzanine area. This section contains numerous examples of Mayan glyphs. Particularly beautiful are the cat glyphs. Also displayed are a vast array of architectural embellishments. Though fragments, these works are exceptional. There are a number of small carved heads in this section and each one is quite different from the others. It is fascinating to look upon these faces carved so long ago and marvel at how very much they look like modern people. One of the most interesting of these pieces portrays the wrinkled face of an old man. In proximity to these human visages are those of gods and demons which are equally thought-provoking. Among the most exquisite works in this section are three Mayan ceramic vessels. Two of these are finely painted and the other is incised. The shorter of the two painted vessels contains beautifully drawn figures. One of the figures on this piece is completely black while the other has a black body but a white face. Body painting was practiced by the Maya as part of their rituals. Victims, for example, were painted blue before being sacrificed. The larger painted vessel is badly damaged but is still quite interesting. The figures on it are skillfully drawn and give insight into Mayan customs. The incised vessel is cylindrical in shape and highly detailed. A Maya personage is gracefully portrayed on this piece which is one of the most interesting in the collection.

Visitor's Choice

The other floors of the CICOM museum are filled with equally curious and fascinating works by the Olmecs, Mayas and numerous other ancient Mexican peoples. Everyone will have personal favorites and the collection is too extensive to single out individual pieces. Of course a few styles which typify certain cultures should be noted so as not to be overlooked.

Pear-Shaped Heads and Almond Eyes

One should not miss any of the small Olmec pieces since each work sheds more light on this little known culture. Especially noteworthy are the small carved pieces with snarling expressions, the carved figurines with pear-shaped heads and almond-shaped eyes and the ceramic figurines. The ceramic figurines seem to represent babies and are about the size of a doll. They have flabby bodies and are portrayed with open legs. Often they are shown sucking a thumb and their hair, or what is possibly a helmet, is reddish in color. Like the carved figurines, the ceramic pieces have a mask-like expression and almond-shaped eyes. The eyes of both styles of figurines have led to speculation about contact between the Olmecs and the ancient Orient but no hard evidence exists to support this idea. Such features may simply reflect those of the Olmecs who like other ancient Americans were descended from Mongoloid stock. Although there are other theories, it is widely held that thousands of years ago humans first entered the Americas from Asia around the area of the Bering Strait.

Ancient Happy Faces

Also not to be missed are the laughing figures from the area of Veracruz. These clay figures are the only ones in ancient Mexico to bear such an expression and no one quite knows why. Perhaps the people who created the thousands of these figures which exist simply had a wonderful sense of humor. Looking at them certainly brings a smile to the faces of most visitors.

Edible Dogs

Note also the small clay dogs from Colima which are quite realistic in their portrayal of canines. In ancient Mexico, many cultures, among them the Aztecs, raised small dogs such as these as a source of food.

Throughout most of Meso-America a ritual ballgame was played and paraphernalia associated with these games is exhibited here and is of great importance. Although numerous pieces have been found which relate to these ancient ballgames no one is quite sure how they were used. Although the rules of these games are not known, it is thought that the losing team was put to death.

Link to the American Southwest

Also of interest are the ceramic pots of the Casas Grandes culture. The beautiful designs of these pots are very similar to those created by native peoples in the area of what is now the southwestern portion of the United States. The Casas Grandes designs are more similar to those of pieces found in the United States than to those of ceramic pots found in other parts of Mexico.

The Insignificance of the Wheel

Finally, one should not overlook a small wheeled toy which is displayed on the last floor of the CICOM museum. This curious piece proves that the wheel was known in ancient America. However, the wheel was only used for toys. Why it was not used for other purposes remains a mystery.

Chapter 10

PALENQUE

The Secret Tomb

Often romatically swathed in mists during the rainy season, Palenque is astonishing to behold at any time of year. Situated atop a hill amid the jungles of the State of Chiapas, a more exotic setting would be hard to imagine.

Though easily reached from Villahermosa by tour bus and, with a bit more effort, by public transportation, perhaps the best way to visit Palenque is by rental car. However, since a driver may encounter large potholes or people and animals in the middle of the road, the trip to Palenque should be made during the day and at an unhurried pace. From Villahermosa, it is a pleasant one-and-a-half to two hours drive to the ruins. Using a rental car allows one total control over a visit to the site and, since there is a great deal to see, a visit of two days is recommended.

For the Explorer

For the more adventuresome traveler, it should be noted that the Mayan ruins of Bonampak and Yaxchilan can be reached by air from Palenque and Villahermosa. Such a trip is, however, expensive. These sites can also be reached from Palenque by a combination of travel by jeep and canoe but the trip is expensive, long and arduous.

Romance of a Jungle Setting

Although the modern town of Palenque is only a few miles from the ruins it holds little of interest for the traveler. There are hotels in the town but the Hotel Chan Kah, currently the closest hotel to the ruins, is probably the best in the region. To further recommend it, some of the finest meals in the area are served in the Chan Kah's restaurant. The hotel consists of a series of individual bungalows situated in a jungle setting. Close to the bungalows is a wonderfully designed swimming pool which contains small rock islands which are perfect for sunbathing. After the drive from Villahermosa or after a day at the ruins, this pool is most inviting. For comfort, food or ambiance, one would be hard put to find the Chan Kah's equal.

Another good choice is the Hotel Mission Palenque which is located five minutes from the ruins. The hotel has air conditioning, a swimming pool and a restaurant. In addition, the Hotel Mission Palenque offers round trip transportation from Villahermosa Airport to Palenque and from the hotel to the ruins.

Essentials for a Memorable Visit

The Mayan ruins of Palenque (open 8 a.m. to 5 p.m. daily) are in the middle of a tropical rainforest and the weather is hot and humid. In such a climate one tires easily. It is, therefore, best to arrive early at the site. One or two hours can be spent in leisurely exploration before returning to one's hotel for lunch and a rest. Late in the afternoon, after the worst heat of the day has passed, one can return to the ruins for further exploration. This procedure can be repeated the following day. Such a plan is also most helpful for photographers since the site will be viewed at times when the play of light and shadow on the buildings is most pronounced.

Furthermore, insect repellent and rubber-soled shoes are strongly recommended for this site. Such shoes are especially important in the early morning when steps and paths are moist with dew. They are essential during the rainy season. A hat is also recommended as is a sun screen for those who are sun-sensitive.

Palenque's Most Famous Attraction

Of all the structures at Palenque, for most visitors, the Temple of the Inscriptions is the most captivating. It is a source of endless fascination for three reasons: the grandeur of its architecture, the inscriptions for which it is named and the tomb deep within.

Architecturally, the Temple of the Inscriptions is one of the most beautifully designed structures to be found anywhere in the world. It consists of a large stepped pyramid surmounted by a temple. A roof comb once adorned this temple but little presently remains of this architectural embellishment which gave this mammoth structure a feeling of lightness and additional height. Although the roof comb on the Temple of the Inscriptions is all but non-existent, there are others at Palenque which are in a much better state of preservation. Though not as steeply inclined as the stairs of some other Mayan temples, those of the Temple of the Inscriptions can be a difficult climb because of the climate. For those who wish to avoid such a climb, but still be able to see the inscriptions as well as the tomb, there is a much easier access via a path behind this structure.

Though named for the inscriptions on the walls of the temple, many of these hieroglyphs are, unfortunately, in poor condition. These glyphs record information about the reign of Lord Pacal, ruler of Palenque, whose tomb the Temple of the Inscriptions houses. The glyphs associate Pacal with the gods and with the sun god in particular. Before descending to Pacal's tomb it is interesting to study some of the hundreds of glyphs which were created in his honor. Also of interest are the stucco reliefs on the columns of the temple which, along with the glyphs, make interesting studies for close-up photography.

Entering the Tomb that Rivaled Tut's

Before Pacal's tomb was discovered in the 1950s, it was believed that, unlike Egyptian pyramids, no Mayan pyramid was ever intended to house a royal tomb. The discovery of this royal tomb within a Mayan pyramid aroused an ever greater interest in this intriguing culture. This interest persists today and shows no signs of abating.

Under the floor of the temple, stairs led to the tomb. Tons of rubble once filled this stairway and had to be painstakingly removed before the burial chamber could be reached. Although the stairway is somewhat steep and can be slippery, a visit to Pacal's final resting place is relatively easy. The effort of navigating these many steps is amply rewarded by the sight of Pacal's stone sarcophagus which is carved in great detail. The lid, in particular, is spectacular. By the size of the sarcophagus and the fact that the stairs leading to it turn back on themselves at a sharp angle, it is obvious that the sarcophagus was set in place first and the pyramid temple was then built over it. A great cache of objects, many of them jade, was found buried with Pacal. These were sent to the National Museum of Anthropology in Mexico City. Furthermore, the remains of six sacrificial victims were found outside the burial chamber.

Great Spot for Photographs and Rest

After ascending from the tomb it is a good idea to rest before any further exploration is attempted. From the top of the Temple of the Inscriptions most of the buildings at Palenque can be seen.

Looking in the direction of the park entrance one sees the remains of Temple XII and two other ruined structures. For the ruin enthusiast a visit to these buildings may be worth a brief visit since Temple XII contains the remains of some stucco ornamentation. However, the average traveler may not consider the climb worth the extra effort since these structures contain little to see and energy can be more profitably spent elsewhere at the site. This vantage point atop the Temple of the Inscriptions also affords a particularly good overview of the Palace complex. Such an overview gives the visitor an idea of the numerous places within the Palace which can be explored.

Unique Mayan Structure

There is much to see in and around the Palace complex and sufficient time should be allotted to wander around this area at a leisurely pace. It is perhaps best to explore this complex on a day other than one on which the Temple of the Inscriptions has been visited.

Though no one is quite sure as to the true function of this complex, it is thought that the Palace was used for administrative purposes. It is known, however, that the various sections of the Palace were added at different periods.

Above the main stairway of the Palace there are columns containing beautiful stucco reliefs. Stucco, however, does not survive well in a moist tropical climate. In 1982 El Chichon erupted covering Palenque with volcanic ash. It is amazing that these reliefs remain at all. Although the reliefs are in full sunlight during the morning hours it may be better to photograph them at a slightly later time since the white reliefs may appear washed out in full sun.

Best Views of Palenque

The most curious aspect of the Palace is the tower. No other Mayan tower exists and its function has only been guessed at. If at all possible, a climb to the top is highly recommended. From this position one not only has a view of most of the structures at Palenque but also a view which stretches for miles across the State of Chiapas. With such a sight range it is easy to agree with those who believe the tower served as a lookout post. However, the tower was most probably used for astronomical observations as well.

Most Beautiful Sculptures in the Americas

Of the many areas to enjoy within the Palace Complex, the Eastern Court is the most beautiful. This courtyard contains some of the most exquisitely executed bas-reliefs to be found anywhere. Carved on large stone slabs, these reliefs portray nine individuals. Who the figures represent and whether or not they are original to Palenque is a matter of debate. The layman, however, can simply enjoy their beauty.

Elongated Heads, Crossed Eyes Signs of Beauty

From the reliefs it is easy to discern the elongated heads which, to the Maya, were a sign of great beauty. In life, this effect was achieved by tying boards to an infant's head. This might seem strange but the Maya also considered crossed eyes a highly desirable attribute and accomplished this by suspending a bead just over the bridge of the nose.

Unique Genital

Although the figures of the reliefs are not carved to normal human proportions they are, perhaps because of this, quite striking and are interesting photographic studies. They are in full sun during mid-afternoon. The relief which attracts the most attention from visitors is one of a male with a monumental penis. This sculpture is on the extreme right.

Hieroglyphs that Photograph Beautifully

Within the same court, directly opposite the large reliefs, is a stairway containing numerous hieroglyphs, only some of which are in good condition. However, those that are intact photograph beautifully. The Hieroglyphic Stairway and the carvings of figures and large glyphs on either side of it are in direct sunlight during the morning hours.

Though smaller than the Eastern Court, the Western Court contains a number of interesting aspects such as additional examples of stucco reliefs. Furthermore, an inspection of the walls in this section reveals some interesting examples of polychromed stucco.

Ruler's Image

Near this court, on a wall just past the tower, is a large stone medallion portraying Lord Pacal and his mother. Pacal, wearing an ornate headdress, earrings, necklace and bracelets, is seated upon a double-headed jaguar whose heads are on opposite ends of its body. Seated in a lower position than her son, Pacal's mother, Lady Zac-Kuk, is offering him an even larger headdress than he is wearing. The headdress represents royal authority. Also clearly discernible on the medallion are a number of glyphs which represent the names of Pacal and his mother. Only a few feet away from this carving and also of interest is a small, rare example of Maya wall painting which should not be missed.

What Most Visitors Miss

Before leaving the Palace Complex, there are two other examples of Mayan art which should not be missed. On the northern facade of the Palace there is a large stucco head as well as other stucco remains. Since these are somewhat out of reach, a telephoto lens or binoculars would be of help. Finally, just beyond the eastern exterior wall of the Palace is a large stone bench referred to as the Palace throne. Since it contains a number of interesting glyphs it is worth closer inspection before moving on to another area of Palenque.

Little Effort Needed

Requiring little effort to see, a visit to the Temple of the Count, the Northern Group and the Palenque Museum would be a good choice after one has visited either the Palace Complex or the Temple of the Inscriptions.

For those who are not ruin enthusiasts, climbing up to the Temple of the Count and to the North Group may not be worthwhile since these structures are not in a particularly good state of preservation.

The Temple of the Count was so named because during the early 1800s a European count supposedly stayed in it while exploring the surrounding ruins. Some of the temple's pyramid base has been restored but little remains of its roof comb or its stucco ornamentation.

The Northern Group consists of a series of temples. Despite the fact that they are in poor condition, they are interesting examples of Maya architecture. They can be seen quite well without climbing up to them.

Directly opposite the North Group are two grass-covered

mounds. Sadly, this is all that remains of Palenque's ball court. While other Mayan sites often contain a number of ball courts, only one court has been found at Palenque.

A welcome haven from the sun, the small museum at the Palenque ruins is well worth the visitor's time. Only a short distance from the North Group, this museum contains numerous artifacts found at this site. Just outside the entrance is the only carved stela ever found at Palenque. It was moved to this spot after being discovered near the Temple of the Cross. Within the museum excellent examples of carved stucco heads, for which Palenque is noted, are displayed along with reliefs, pottery, a mosaic jade mask, many fine examples of glyphs and other interesting artifacts.

Tips On Four Mayan Masterpieces

Four other structures which should not be missed at Palenque are the Temple of the Sun, Temple XIV, the Temple of the Cross and the Temple of the Foliated Cross. To reach these buildings it is necessary to cross the Otolum River which runs through Palenque and which supplied its water. This small river, which should be more aptly termed a creek, is crossed by means of a log which serves as a bridge. For those wishing to photograph these four temples, visiting this area at two different times of day would be worth considering. The Temple of the Sun and Temple XIV face east, the Temple of the Cross faces south and the Temple of the Foliated Cross faces west.

Of the four structures, the Temple of the Sun is the most complete. Its roof comb is almost completely intact and remnants of a stucco frieze can be seen on the roof just below it. Remains of other stucco work can be seen on the columns of this temple as well.

Ancient Portraits

Within this exquisite, small temple are three bas-reliefs. The large, central relief is in fairly good condition and is highly detailed. In the center of this relief is a shield and two crossed spears. These seem to be on an altar which is supported on the backs of two figures. The shield is flanked by two humans which are standing on the backs of two other figures. Furthermore, these humans each hold a small figure in their upturned hands. Besides the shield and the eight figures, this relief also contains a great quantity of glyphs and other embellishments.

Unfortunately, only fragments remain of the two sections on either side of the center relief. What does remain of these is, however, beautiful.

Maya Fashion

To the right of the Temple of the Sun stands what remains of Temple XIV. This temple is in poor condition but it should not be bypassed since it, too, houses an extremely interesting bas-relief. Though it is cracked and fragments are missing, the majority of the images on this relief remain. In a standing position on the right side of this plaque is a ruler of Palenque. He wears an extensive headdress, earrings, necklace, bracelets, a highly decorative loincloth, and anklets. Kneeling before this figure is a richly costumed Maya noblewoman. In her upraised hands she holds the small figure of a god. This relief is also extensively carved with hieroglyphs.

Breathtaking Views

Another reason for visiting Temple XIV is the excellent perspective afforded from its pyramid base of the Palace and the Temple of the Inscriptions to the west.

Although the relief from which it derives its name was moved to the National Museum of Anthropology in Mexico City, the climb to the Temple of the Cross is well worth the effort. Two smaller reliefs, which are finely carved and in a good state of preservation, are still in place. Furthermore, from this vantage point the overall views of Palenque and, in particular, of Temple XIV and the Temple of the Sun are breathtaking.

An Unusual Cross

As with the Temple of the Cross, the Temple of the Foliated Cross is missing its facade. Situated on a hill amid lush foliage, this temple once contained three bas-reliefs. Only fragments remain of the two side reliefs but the center relief is, for the most part, intact. Besides the highly embellished central cross, this relief portrays two human figures and numerous other interesting details and glyphs.

The structures which can currently be visited at Palenque

comprise what is referred to as the ceremonial center. However, the ancient city of Palenque extended for some miles into the jungle. Many of its buildings have yet to be fully explored and others remain undiscovered.

Palenque's Most Exotic Locale

For an idea of what many Meso-American ruins looked like prior to their restoration, a visit to the Temple of the Lion is recommended before completing one's tour of the Palenque ruins.

Behind and to the left of the Temple of the Inscriptions, a short path leads through the jungle to this small temple. Though the temple is overgrown with vegetation and is in extremely poor condition, it still evokes a sense of adventure and romance. From this spot, through a break in the jungle canopy, the roof comb of the Temple of the Sun can be seen in the distance. It is the only other human creation which can be seen from this location.

Dappled by sunlight piercing the jungle, except for the rush of the Otolum River below and the cries of birds above, the Temple of the Lion stands alone in silence.

Great Intellect And Blood Sacrifices

For many centuries the other structures at Palenque, abandoned before the arrival of Europeans, also stood covered by jungle. No one is certain why Palenque and other Mayan cities were abandoned but many theories have been offered such as disease, soil depletion, crop failure, drought or a change in climate. It may have been a combination of these things or it may be that the Maya simply tired of the ever increasing demands of their priests and rulers. We may never know with any certainty if Maya society declined because of outside forces or because of political, social and religious struggles. However, we do know a number of facts about this once great culture. The Maya had a system of picture writing; they could count and figure; they had the concept of zero long before Europeans did; they could accurately predict the movements of heavenly bodies and had a calendar more accurate than our own. Furthermore, it is known that the Maya had definite religious beliefs concerning the universe and their gods. On a more somber note, as part of their beliefs the Maya engaged in bloodletting rituals in which a cord with thorns was passed through the tongue or obsidian knives, thorns, or stringray spines were used to pierce the ears, nose, lips or sexual organs. Although animals were sacrificed, most shocking is the fact that a human life was considered essential for the continued well-being of the gods.

It is hard for the mind to reconcile the high minded achievements of the Maya with some of their violent practices but perhaps all that need be said is that they were human.

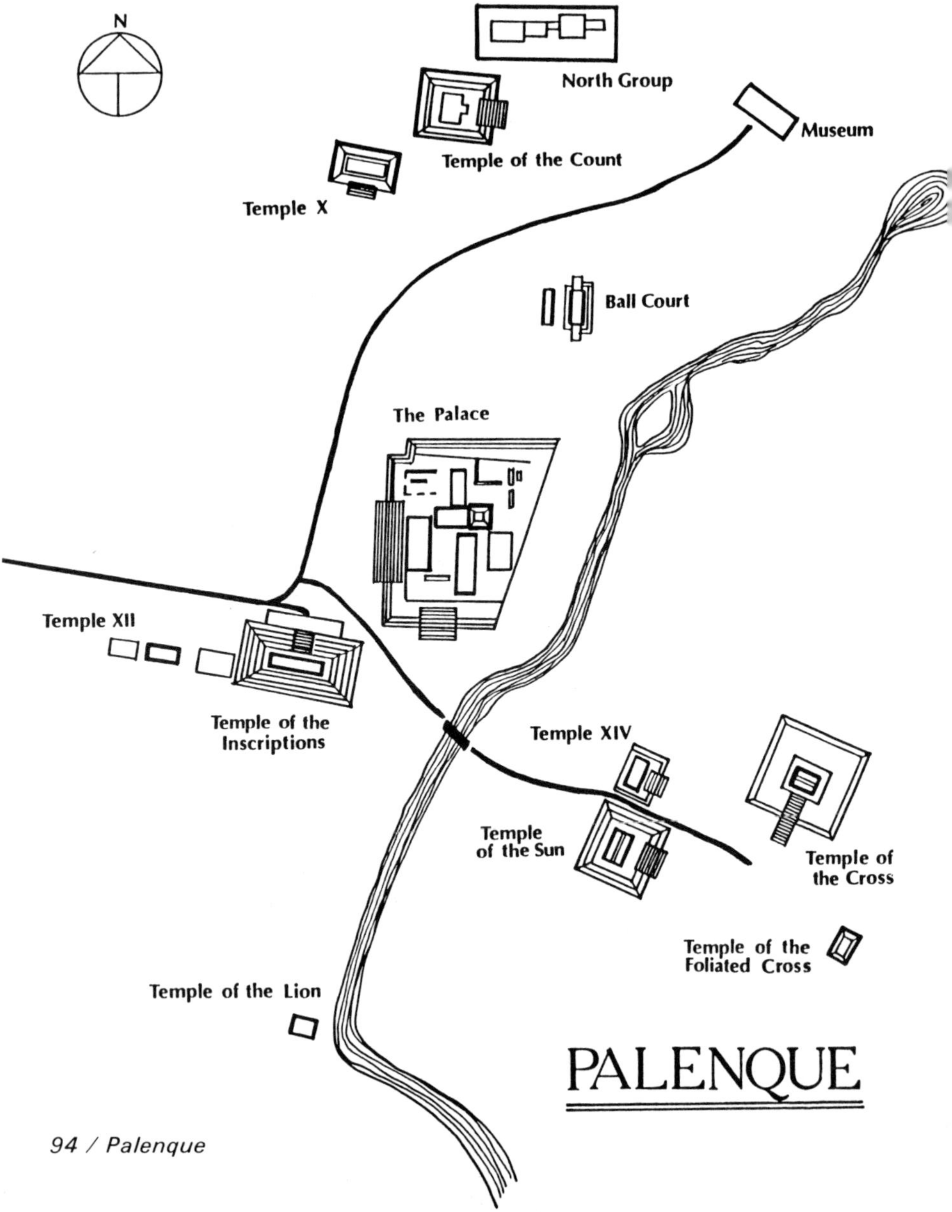

Chapter 11

THE YUCATAN PENINSULA

The Newest Destination

The Yucatan Peninsula is comprised of the Mexican states of Campeche, Yucatan and Quintana Roo. To the west of the peninsula is the Gulf of Mexico and to the east, the Caribbean Sea.

Now Easy to Reach

Once difficult to reach, today this area is one of the most visited parts of Mexico. Modern highways and the advent of jet travel have made the Yucatan Peninsula easy to explore. Besides numerous Mayan ruins, this area contains interesting cities, such as Campeche and Merida, as well as luxury resorts such as Cancun.

Vacation Variety

Depending on one's interest and the time one has available, it is possible to visit just one place on the Yucatan Peninsula or to visit many. Campeche, on the west coast of the peninsula, Merida, in the north, and Cancun, on the east coast, afford a wide variety of accommodations and the best access to this area. For those wishing the romance of exotic surroundings, it is possible to relax at comfortable and luxurious accommodations at the strangely beautiful Mayan ruins of Uxmal, Chichen Itza and Coba.

Why People Come

Travelers come to the Yucatan Peninsula for the glorious beaches of Cancun and Cozumel and because this was a center of Mayan culture. The Yucatan Peninsula affords the traveler the opportunity of enjoying good food, fine hotels, and water sports as well as the adventure and intellectual stimulation of exploring the ruined cities of a somewhat enigmatic people. Ever increasing numbers of people, from diverse backgrounds, come to the Yucatan Peninsula to satisfy their curiosity about the Maya who built magnificent cities of stone and then abandoned them. It is easy to believe that the Coliseum, the Acropolis and even the great pyramids of Egypt were built by humans. The Mayan builders, however, seem somehow more than human. Perhaps because they stand alone, far from modern cities, the cities built by the Mayans have a mystic quality. This, to a great degree, is why they fascinate all who behold them.

Mysterious Maya

What we know of the Maya themselves has come down to us through their few remaining bark paper books, their hieroglyphs, their art, and from works written shortly after the Spanish Conquest.

The Maya were a people governed by their religious beliefs and ruled by their priests. For the Maya, who believed in thirteen heavens and nine hells, a person's destiny after death was determined more by the manner of death than by conduct during life.

It is generally believed that the Maya slowly migrated to the Yucatan Peninsula from the Pacific coast of what is today Honduras and Guatemala. As with all people, Mayan beliefs were influenced by the natural world they saw around them. The jaguar, for example, was revered as Lord of the Jungle and was associated with royalty and with the gods. The serpent, the quetzal bird, the vulture, the frog, the crocodile and bees, all part of the Maya environment, had a place in Mayan belief and symbolism.

Everywhere about them in Nature the Maya saw the power of their gods. The gods had given them life and they owed these gods a debt. The Maya feared this power and the priests exploited this fear. Even the Maya creation story contained an example of what happened to those who failed to praise the creators.

The Maya Creation

For the Maya, only silence and calm existed before the world was brought into being. All that existed was a motionless sea and a vast, empty sky. All was darkness except for the Creators who were enveloped in light. At the proper moment, the Creators enjoined the emptiness to be filled. The earth came forth from the waters where, the Maya believed, it rested on the back of a great crocodile. Then the Creators made all the creatures of the land and the water and the air. The Creators were very disappointed, however, for their creations could only utter strange sounds and could not praise their makers. It was then that the gods decided to make humans. The first attempt was a failure because the clay the gods used crumbled in the water. The gods next made people out of wood. These could jabber and reproduce but they, having neither mind nor soul, forgot to worship their creators. Because of this, the gods destroyed them. The gods caused everything the wooden people had offended to rise up against them. Next, a great flood was ordained. Those few people who survived the deluge turned into monkeys. At last, with the help of the animals, the gods formed four men from plants. These men knew almost as much as the gods. As the men became prideful, the gods became worried and decided that the knowledge of these men should be limited. The men were then given wives and from these people the Maya believed they were descended.

A Debt of Blood

The Maya felt a heavy obligation to sustain the gods who had created and nourished them. To the Maya, the sacrifice of living beings was immanently logical. Daily, the Maya saw enacted the natural law that in order for one creature to live another living thing, be it plant or animal, had to be eaten. This is as true for humans as it is for animals. Could the needs of the gods be any different? The Maya sacrificed a variety of animals including iguanas, crocodiles, jaguars, dogs and turkeys. Offerings were either freshly killed or cooked. Sometimes just the hearts were offered. However, a fundamental tenet of Mayan belief was that human blood was the indispensable sustenance of the gods. As the apex of creation, humans were the most perfect sacrifice. Slaves, captured enemy soldiers, illegitimate children, orphans and criminals were among those offered to the gods. When necessary, children were bought or stolen from other cities. Some victims were volunteers since to be sacrificed was considered a great honor. All victims were stripped and painted blue but the manner of sacrifice varied. Some victims had their chest cut open at the top of a pyramid and their still beating heart was ripped out and offered to the gods. Victims were also sacrificed by decapitation, disembowelment, hanging, drowning or beating. Some were even sacrificed by dancers who shot arrows into the victim's heart.

The Maya also practiced many forms of bloodletting, offering the gods their own blood. This they felt obligated to do.

Until this century, it was believed that, before they were

conquered by the Toltecs, the Maya did not practice human sacrifice. As is now known, this is not true. Mayan art, such as the murals of Bonampak, clearly show that the Maya practiced human sacrifice before the Toltec invasion. Perhaps it was not practiced on as great a scale as after Toltec domination but, nonetheless, it was the custom.

Unique Travel Destination

More than anything else, it is this ancient culture which attracts thousands of travelers to the Yucatan Peninsula each year. Other places can offer excellent cuisine, exceptional hotels and beaches which seem to stretch endlessly. However, the Yucatan Peninsula offers all these pleasures plus the wonder and romance of a lost civilization.

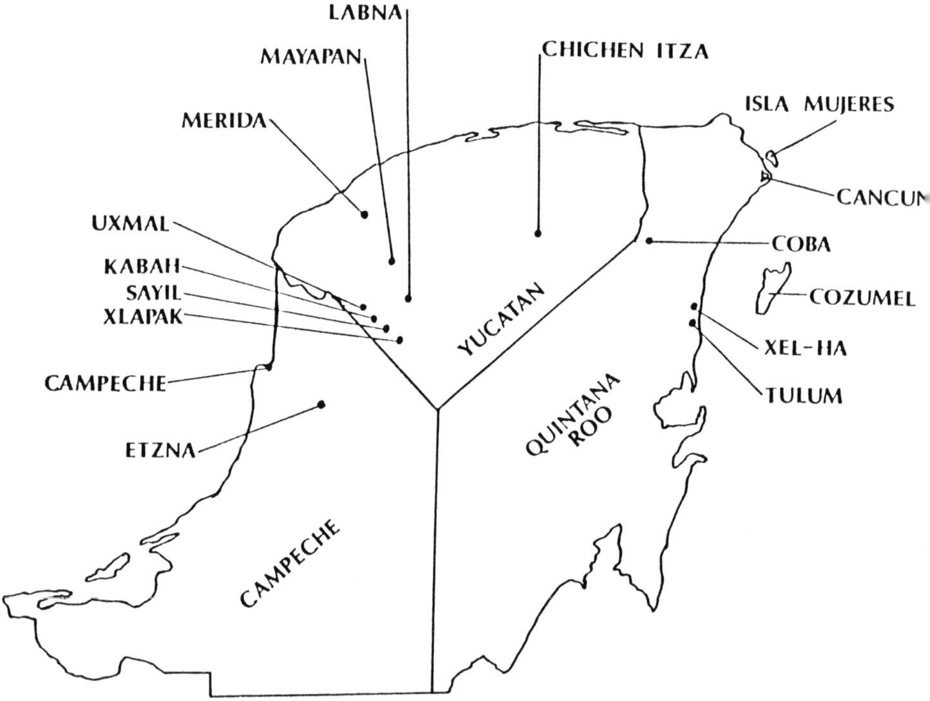

THE YUCATAN PENINSULA

Chapter 12
CAMPECHE and MERIDA
Two Colonial Charmers

The cities of Campeche and Merida lie at opposite ends of Route 261. Along this route are numerous archaeological sites. Another highway, Route 180, also connects the two cities and shortens traveling time considerably. However, the shorter route bypasses all of the region's important archaeological zones.

Both Campeche and Merida are excellent places to begin or end a trip through the Yucatan Peninsula. There is airline service to both cities from within Mexico. However, there are far more flights to and from Merida than Campeche and only Merida has international flights.

Relaxing But Overlooked

Of the two cities, Campeche is less likely to be visited by most travelers to the Yucatan. The city is the capital of the state of Campeche and is directly on the Gulf of Mexico. In spite of its proximity to this body of water, Campeche has no beaches suitable for either swimming or for sunbathing. The Gulf of Mexico does, however, provide Campeche with an abundance of seafood for which it is famous.

Except for the two branches of the Museum of Anthropology, there is little to see in Campeche. Furthermore, during the day it is extremely hot and humid. The cool breezes off the Gulf of Mexico are lost as soon as one walks inland even a few streets. Campeche is a colonial city built behind Mayan walls. Many of the walls and their fortresses still exist and can be visited. However, this should be done in the early morning or the late afternoon to avoid as much of Campeche's heat and humidity as possible.

Visitors who do come to Campeche are usually those who wish to visit the nearby ruins of Etzna. Generally, only one night is spent in Campeche and that is unfortunate. Even though Campeche does not have an abundance of tourist attractions, the city can provide a relaxing interlude on a trip through Mexico. The people of Campeche are pleasant and helpful and the sunsets over the

Gulf of Mexico are spectacular. One of the most pleasant ways to spend time in Campeche is to take a walk along the water at sunset.

A Superior Hotel

For those wishing to relax, a stay at Campeche's Hotel El Presidente provides almost everything a tired traveler could desire. Located only a few feet from the Gulf of Mexico, the hotel offers beautiful, spacious rooms, each of which has a terrace, air conditioning and cable TV. The hotel's water is purified, its restaurants serve good food and it has a swimming pool.

From the Hotel El Presidente, those wishing to do so can easily explore Campeche on foot. However, to visit the ruins of Etzna, or to travel to Uxmal, a car is necessary. Travelers should be aware that it is difficult to rent a car with automatic transmission in Campeche. Cars with automatic transmissions can be requested but cannot be guaranteed.

Charming Colonial City

Unlike Campeche, Merida is visited by many travelers because of its proximity to Chichen Itza and to Uxmal and its neighboring sites. Merida, capital of the state of Yucatan, is a charming colonial city. Although there are not a great many things to do in Merida, the city's charm, its nearness to major archaeological sites and the interesting shopping it offers make it popular with travelers.

Intimate and Very Special

One of the best ways to experience some of Merida's charm is to stay at the Hotel Casa Del Balam. This small hotel, located at Calle 60 no. 488, is near the main plaza. The hotel is built around a small courtyard and, in an adjoining walled garden, there is a swimming pool. Rooms are spacious and all are air conditioned. The hotel also has a restaurant, a bar and a travel agency. This beautiful colonial-style hotel is affiliated with the Hotel Mayaland at Chichen Itza and with the Hacienda Uxmal. All three are among Mexico's very special hotels.

Those not driving can arrange tours to Chichen Itza, Uxmal and also to Kabah, Sayil, Xlapak and Labna through the Merida Travel Service which is located in the lobby of the Hotel Casa Del Balam.

Nearby Restaurant

A short distance from the Hotel Casa Del Balam is Restaurante Portico del Peregrino. Located at Calle 57 no. 501, this restaurant is one of the finest in Merida. One can dine in a small courtyard or in the air-conditioned dining rooms. The restaurant's decor is charming, the food is excellent and the waiters are helpful and attentive.

Two Good Breakfast Choices

For a good, inexpensive breakfast, try Cafeteria Pop next to Portico del Peregrino on Calle 57. Also try Panificadora Montejo, on the Zocalo at the corner of Calle 62 and Calle 63, which sells delicious breads and sweet rolls. However, no beverages are sold at Panificadora Montejo.

Surviving Merida's Market

Besides sightseeing and good food, many visitors also enjoy shopping in Merida. Those interested in shopping usually head for the market which is not necessarily the best place to make purchases. The quality of the goods sold at the market varies widely and the vendors tend to be much more aggressive than in other parts of Mexico. Many merchants are persistent and quite persuasive. Those who are easily swayed should be very careful in the market. When one says *"No, gracias"* to an offer to take a closer look, it must be clear that one means what one is saying. This is best achieved by a firm tone of voice, a serious facial expression and by simply walking away.

Living Jewelry

A great variety of goods can be bought at the market—from the usual blankets and shirts to the more exotic, and even bizarre. The most unusual items to be sold at the market are "living jewels." This jewelry is actually large beetles which have been encrusted with gold colored paint and fake jewels. The living beetles are attached to a shirt or blouse by means of a small chain.

Buying a Hammock

Those seeking something less eccentric can purchase hammocks of the finest quality in Merida. They are sold in the market and by numerous street vendors. However, hammocks come in three sizes and, also, quality varies. Unless one is extremely knowledgeable about hammocks, it makes more sense to buy them in a reputable shop such as La Poblana, S.A. at Calle 65 no. 492.

Where to Find Local Crafts

Although the Yucatan is not noted for its handicrafts, an attempt is being made to promote the work of local crafts people. Shoppers wishing to purchase Yucatecan handicrafts, as well as those from other parts of Mexico, should visit La Casa de La Cultura at Calle 63 no. 513 and El Museo Regional de Artesania, behind La Majorado Convent, on Calle 59. La Casa de La Cultura is open Monday to Friday, 9 a.m. to 7:30 p.m. The Museo Regional de Artesania is open Tuesday to Saturday from 8 a.m. to 8 p.m., and on Sunday from 9 a.m. to 2 p.m.

More About the Maya

If time permits, visit the Museo Regional de Antropologia which is on the Paseo de Montejo at the corner of Calle 43. The museum is housed in a magnificent mansion built in the early 1900s. For those interested in learning more about the Maya, the Anthropological Museum is a must. It is open Tuesday to Saturday from 8 a.m. to 8 p.m., and Sundays from 8 a.m. to 2 p.m.

The Yucatan Peninsula offers travelers a multitude of travel possibilities. It is exotic but still provides most of the amenities that travelers enjoy. Modern roads between Merida and Campeche have made this area of Mexico accessible to more travelers than ever before and both cities are pleasant and convenient places from which to explore the Yucatan's many sights.

Chapter 13

ETZNA

Rarely Seen Magnificence

There are only a few structures to see at Etzna but it is, nonetheless, one of the most beautiful of Mexico's archaeological sites. Rarely visited by tourists, Etzna, also known as Edzna, can be reached on a long day trip from Uxmal. However, this is not the best way of visiting the site. Ideally, Etzna should be visited on a day trip from the city of Campeche or it can be visited as one drives from Campeche to Uxmal. The site is open from 8 a.m. to 5 p.m. daily and is located forty-one miles from the city of Campeche. Etzna is easily reached provided one is on Route 261. It is easy to get on the wrong highway when leaving Campeche and, if this happens, finding one's way to Etzna can be extremely difficult and frustrating. It is essential to get directions to Route 261 before leaving Campeche.

Just past the entrance to the Etzna site is a carved stele, in good condition, which bears the image of a Mayan lord. Directly across from this carved stone slab is a small temple. Unfortunately, little more than a platform, stairs and a few columns remain of this structure.

A Revelation

Etzna's Great Plaza is located a short distance from the temple and is reached by means of a large stone stairway. As one reaches the top stairs, the plaza's focal point, the Pyramid of the Five Stories, is revealed. There are four other structures built around the plaza and three have been well restored. Like the pyramid, these structures are of a stepped design and climbing them provides excellent views of the pyramid.

Many Many Photographic Possibilities

The most impressive structure at Etzna, the Pyramid of the Five Stories is a large, stepped structure with five levels. An exterior, central stairway gives access to the pyramid's main rooms as well as to the top story which consists of a temple with a beautiful roof comb. The lower steps of the stairway contain exquisite Mayan glyphs which are ideal subjects for close-up photography. The Pyramid of the Five Stories faces west and should be visited during afternoon hours when its five levels receive the best lighting.

Although there are not many structures remaining at Etzna, the Pyramid of the Five Stories and the design of the Great Plaza are truly magnificent. Those wishing to see an extraordinary and relatively overlooked Mayan site should consider adding Etzna to their itinerary.

ETZNA

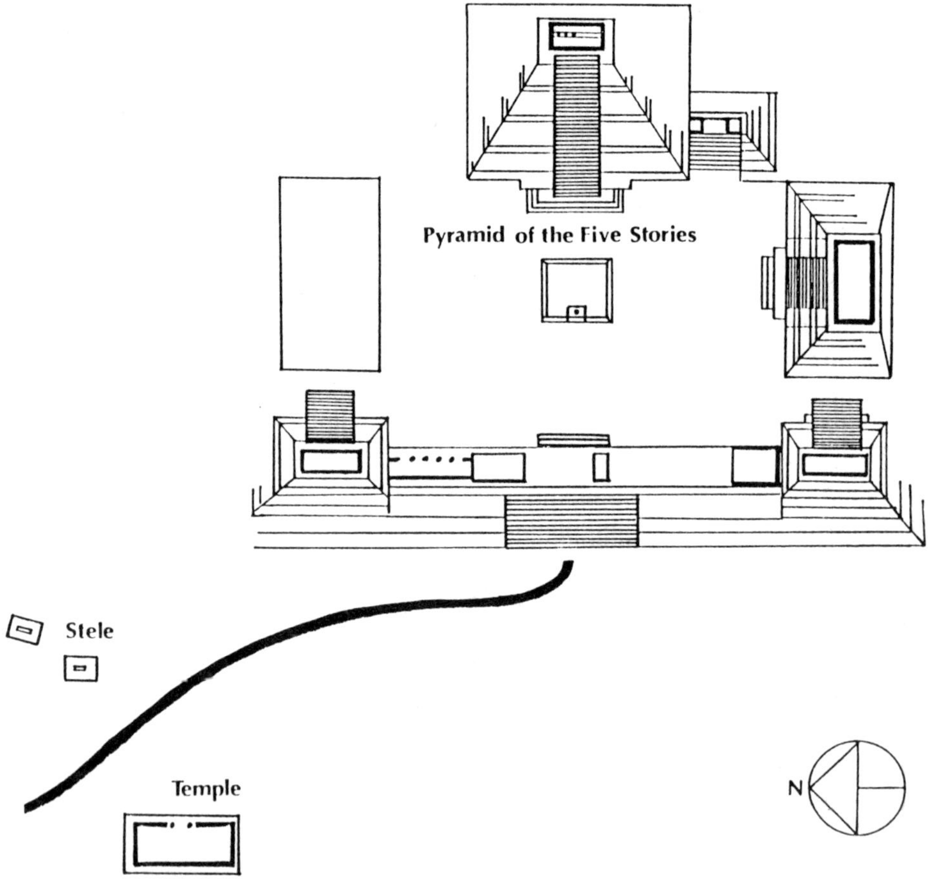

Chapter 14

UXMAL

Most Beautiful of Mayan Cities

Though overshadowed by Chichen Itza, its more famous neighbor, and considered by some to be less beautiful than Palenque, a strong case can be made for Uxmal as the Crown Jewel of Mayan cities. The ruins are open daily from 8 a.m. to 5 p.m.

This spectacular site can easily be reached using Campeche or Merida as a base. An interesting trip would be to start from Campeche and work one's way to Merida. Between the two cities there are so many Mayan sites that for the Mayan enthusiast such a trip could be called the Golden Route.

Making the Most Out of a Visit to Uxmal

Most visitors who come to Uxmal do so on a day trip from Merida, not from Campeche. However, if one is coming to Uxmal from Merida, a stay of two or more nights near the ruins would allow ample opportunity to see Uxmal as well as the opportunity to see one or more of the neighboring ruins of Kabah, Sayil, Xlapak, Labna or Mayapan. Although the major structures at Uxmal can be seen in one day, a visit to this area should not be a hurried one. There are a number of fine hotels at or near the site which provide comfortable accommodations amid luxurious surroundings.

Hotel with Aerial Acrobats

Of the hotels near Uxmal, the Hacienda Uxmal is especially charming and tranquil. Built in the Spanish style around a central courtyard, the hotel, which is directly across the road from the ruins, is beautifully decorated and the rooms are spacious and attractively furnished. Amid lush tropical vegetation, a pool is the centerpiece of the courtyard. Besides being most inviting after a day of visiting the ruins, the swimming pool area provides a close view of the numerous small birds which come to quench their thirst here. Happily sharing the pool with hotel guests, the birds perform spectacular aerial maneuvers as they swoop down to the water and drink while in flight. Most numerous in late afternoon, the birds are marvelously entertaining airborne acrobats. As night descends the birds, seemingly on signal, leave.

Just outside the entrance to the ruins is a Villas Arqueologicas hotel. Since it is basically identical to other Villas Arqueologicas hotels, one is assured of comfortable accommodations in pleasant surroundings.

Most Enchanting Light and Sound Show

When visiting Uxmal one should see the sound and light show which is presented each night at the ruins (9 p.m. in English). It is best to see this show before exploring the ruins. Although the dialogue which accompanies the lighting effects is trite and the lighting on most of the buildings is similar to other sound and light shows, the visual effects on the Nunnery Quadrangle are spectacular. The structures which make up the quadrangle contain a profusion of details which visitors often do not notice because, in daylight, these details appear as white designs on a white background. During the sound and light show spectators are seated on the north side of the Nunnery Quadrangle and can clearly see the highlighting of the architectural details. This makes it easy to find them during the day.

Uxmal now has a small museum and this is how visitors enter the site. The museum contains carvings and pottery found at Uxmal and in the courtyard there is a model of the Nunnery Quadrangle.

Built by Magic

The first structure one comes upon at Uxmal is the massive Pyramid of the Magician. Oval in shape this building was, according to myth, built in a single night by a magical child who had been brought forth from an egg by a witch. This child grew to adulthood in a year and through a series of magical feats, one of which was the building of the pyramid, became Lord of Uxmal. However, since there are a number of earlier constructions which can be seen within the pyramid, it is hard to understand how such a legend came about.

The climb to the top of the Pyramid of the Magician is an exhilarating experience except for those with a fear of heights. This is especially true if one uses the stairs on the east side, which is the rear of the structure. If one looks down after reaching the top there is the impression, due to the angle of inclination, that there are no steps. One has the illusion of stepping out into space with death being imminent. However, one can, if one wishes, descend the steps sitting down, clinging to the chain provided.

Yucatan's Most Spectacular Panorama

At the top of the pyramid's west side one has a panoramic view of most of the major structures at Uxmal. In particular one has an exceptional overview of the entire Nunnery Quadrangle. From this vantage point the symmetry of the Nunnery can be appreciated in a way that is not possible from ground level.

Uxmal's Most Necessary God

The stairs on the west side of the Pyramid of the Magician are less difficult to descend than those on the east side but one must still be very careful. These stairs lead to a temple which one enters through the mouth of a giant mask. The facade of the temple is covered with representations of the rain god, Chaac. The god Chaac was very important at Uxmal since rain was the only source of water for the city. Rain was seasonal, and it was necessary for the inhabitants of Uxmal to catch and save rain water for use during the long dry periods. To do this numerous *chultunes* were created. These cisterns can still be seen at Uxmal and at nearby sites such as Sayil. From this temple the stairs, which are flanked by Chaac masks, lead to ground level.

Representations of Chaac are found throughout Uxmal and many of the finest can be seen in the Nunnery Quadrangle which is just a short distance from the Pyramid of the Magician.

A Nunnery Without Nuns

The Nunnery was so named because this is what it looked like to the Spanish. To date, no one really knows what purpose the buildings served. The Nunnery is a complex of four separate buildings each containing different and very beautiful architectural detailing. The complex is entered through a Mayan or corbeled arch in the South Building. Within the arch there are red hand prints. They are hard to discern but are, nonetheless, fascinating because no one knows why they are there. Such an arch was formed at a desired point by stepping each successive layer of masonry inward. The two sides were then joined by a keystone, thus creating an inverted V shaped opening. Although the Maya never used a true arch, what they created was functional and visually pleasing.

The Serpent on the Wall

Standing in the courtyard formed by the four structures which make up the Nunnery, it is possible to view the numerous architectural details which adorn these buildings. Besides the arch, the south building is adorned with small Mayan thatched roofed huts, masks of the god Chaac and lattice designs which are all of carved stone. The facade of the north building also contains representations of Mayan huts as well as serpents with heads at both ends, geometric designs and tiers of Chaac masks. Although the facades of these buildings are beautiful, those of the west building and of the east building are even more exquisitely detailed. The west building contains beautiful geometric designs and a human figure. However, the most interesting detail of this structure is the great serpent on the western facade. Winding across the building, the serpent's body doubles back on itself and the rattle and head almost meet. Directly opposite this structure is the east building. Of the four Nunnery buildings, the facade of the east building is the most strikingly symmetrical. The corners contain tiers of hooked nosed Chaac masks and such masks are to be seen again at the center of the facade. On both sides of the central tier of masks there are six groups of serpent designs each of which is surmounted by an owl. Each group contains eight serpents which have a head at both ends of the body and the serpent groupings are separated by lattice designs.

The four facades which can be seen from the Nunnery courtyard are masterpieces of architectural detailing. Because of their visual beauty much time can be pleasantly spent in this area of the Nunnery viewing and photographing the many interesting decorations. Perhaps because of the orderliness of its layout, the Nunnery seems to exhude an air of tranquility which is hard to leave.

Beyond the Nunnery is a ball court which has yet to be fully restored and is, therefore, of far less interest than the one at Chichen Itza. However, one can see the remains of a stone ring used in the games played here.

Facing the ball court is a small building known as the Temple or

House of the Turtles. It was thus named because of the small carvings of turtles which adorn it. Noted for its simplicity, the Temple of the Turtles is beautiful in an understated way.

Tour de Force in Stone

Of all the structures at Uxmal, perhaps the most superlative adjectives have been lavished upon the Palace of the Governor. The proportions and details of the building are unsurpassed. The lower level of the structure is completely unadorned while the upper level is covered in magnificent detail work. Among the details are serpents, Chaac masks, lattice designs, the figure of a Mayan ruler and a geometric design resembling a bent index finger. The Palace of the Governor also contains excellent examples of the corbeled arch. Those in this structure resemble huge arrows. The best of these arches is found in the south section of the front facade. There is a small platform in front of the Palace and this is the best spot from which to take photographs of the building. The detailing is best illuminated in the morning.

What the Guides Never Show

Though now mostly in ruin, the Great Pyramid or Dwarf's House is another interesting structure at Uxmal. Restoration is fairly recent and little more than the large stairway has been reconstructed. Although a great deal of the Great Pyramid looks like little more than a pile of rubble, it gives the visitor an idea of the condition to which most pre-Columbian sites had deteriorated. A climb to the top of this structure is recommended for the superb view and to see the details of the pyramid's temple. Among these are an extremely large Chaac mask which is just inside the temple's entrance. The corners of this temple consist of tiers of Chaac masks and from under the large noses of these masks small faces peer out.

Remarkable Show of Light and Shadow

Not far from the Great Pyramid are the remains of a structure known as the House of the Dove-Cotes which derives its name from the fact that its roof comb resembles a dove shelter. Roof combs were used by the Maya to architecturally create an added sense of height and a feeling of lightness. Although in a poor state of preservation, the House of the Dove-Cotes is nonetheless interesting for its visual beauty. At various times of the day, the play of light and shadow on the roof comb is remarkable.

There are other structures at Uxmal, such as those of the cemetery group and the north group, but they are less accessible and of less interest to the layman. After visiting the major buildings it is perhaps best to simply wander at will, stopping where one's interest or fancy dictates.

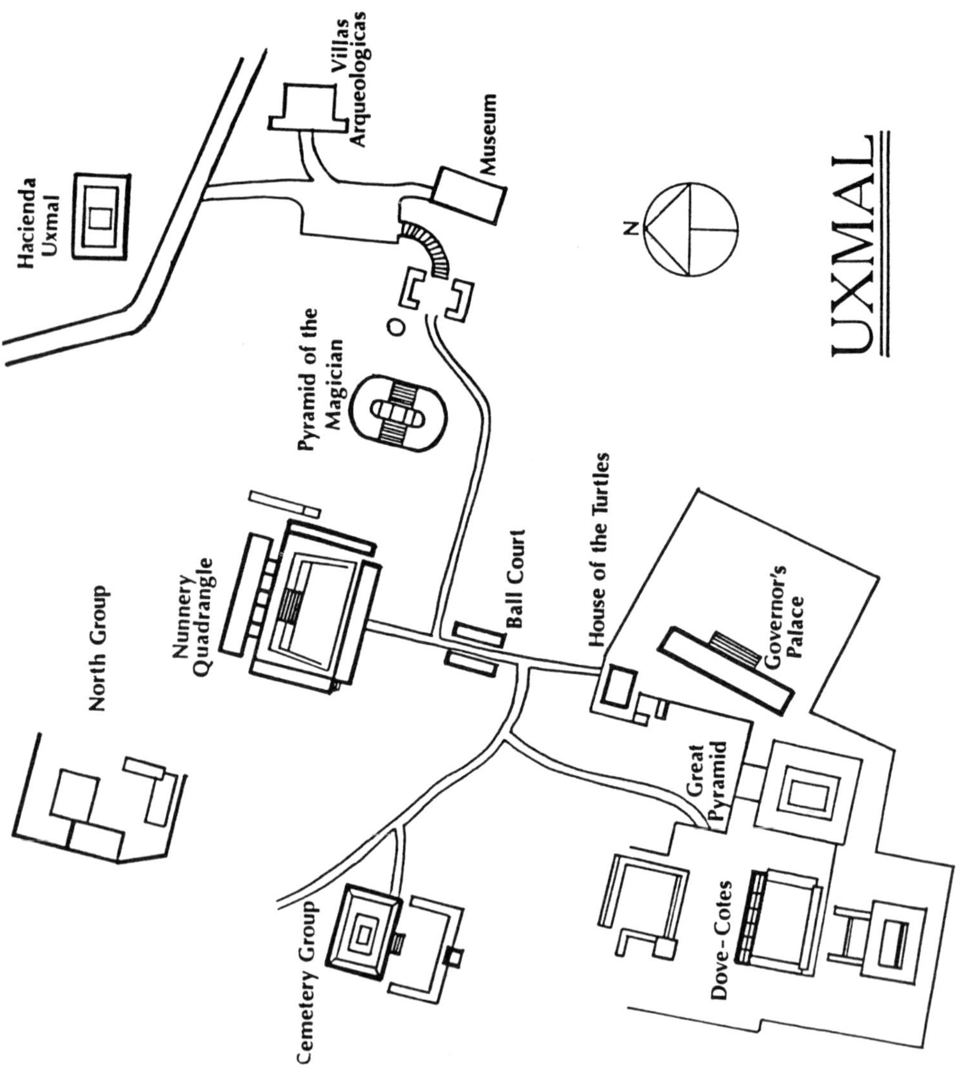

Chapter 15

KABAH, SAYIL, XLAPAK and LABNA

Infinite Photographic Possibilities

Anyone wishing to see some of the most beautiful and most unusual architecture in the world should make an effort to visit Kabah, Sayil, Xlapak and Labna. All four sites are open from 8 a.m. to 5 p.m. daily. Most people visit all four sites on a long day trip from Uxmal. However, they can also be visited as one drives from Campeche to Merida via Route 261 which is known as the long route. Each of the four ruin sites has its own distinctive character and each offers numerous photographic opportunities.

Closest to Uxmal

Of the four sites, Kabah is the closest to Uxmal. It is approximately fourteen miles farther south on Route 261 which passes directly through Kabah and which divides the site into two sections. Kabah's most famous structures, the Palace and the Codz Poop, are located east of the highway and the Kabah Arch is located west of the highway.

The Palace is an extremely plain building. Its first level is unrestored but one can see the remains of a large stairway in this area. The second level is in much better condition. There are seven doorways in the facade of this level and two of these portals have a column in their center. Above the doorways, and running the length of the facade, is a frieze containing small, decorative columns. Except for the remnants of a roof comb atop the Palace, there are no other decorative details.

Noses as Steps

By comparison, the Codz Poop is a riot of architectural detail. The facade of this structure is covered with over two hundred masks of the god Chaac. The supposed resemblance of the masks' curved noses to rolled mats is the reason the structure is called the Codz Poop. The Mayan words for rolled mats are codz poop. Unfortunately, most of the noses are partially or completely broken. Many of the pieces can be seen arranged in rows in front

KABAH

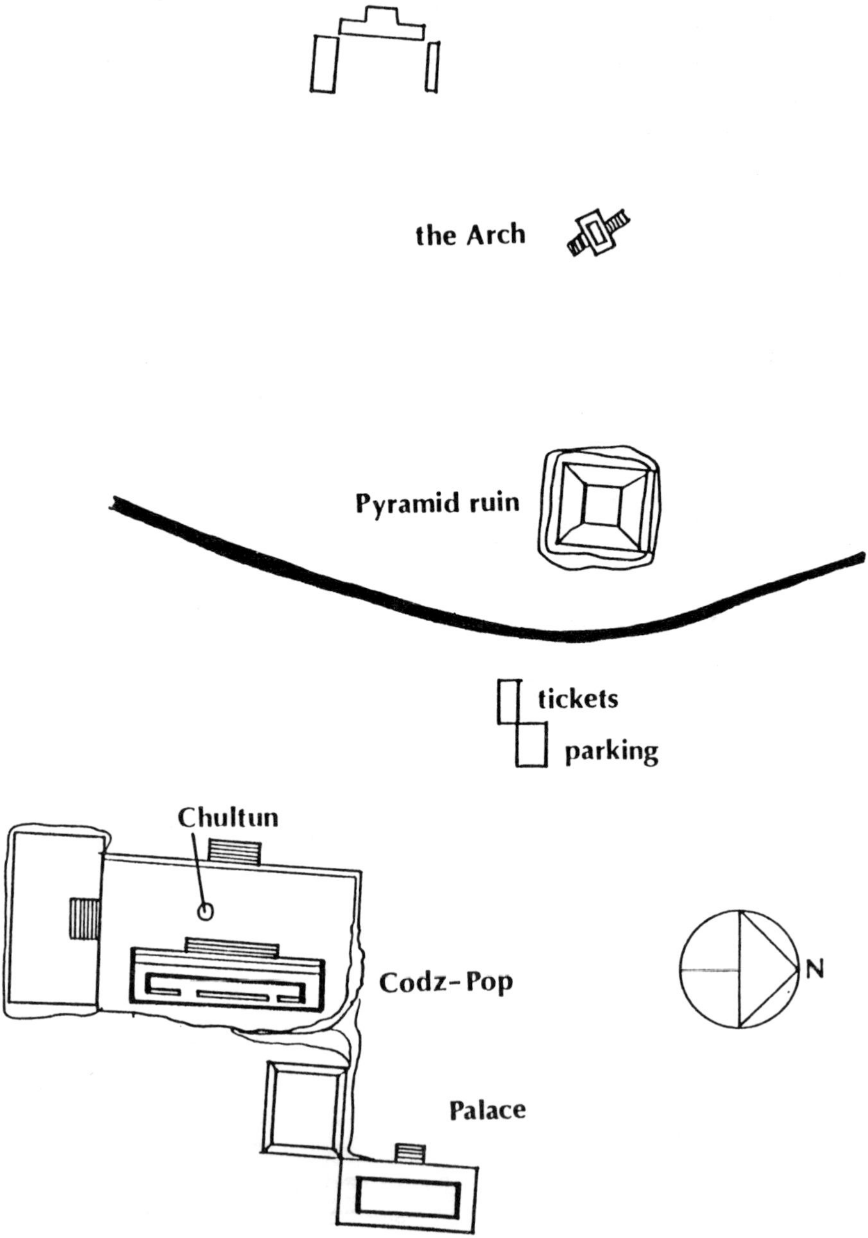

the Arch
Pyramid ruin
tickets
parking
Chultun
Codz-Pop
Palace
N

of the Codz Poop. It is hoped that one day they will be restored to the facade. Some of the most interesting and most complete masks can be found under the Codz Poop's doorways where the noses serve as steps. In front of the Codz Poop, which is also known as the Palace of the Masks, a platform bears some interesting Mayan glyphs and nearby there is also a *chultun.*

A Rarely Visited Area

On the west side of the highway a wide path leads to Kabah's Arch. From the beginning of this path one has an overview of the structures on the east side of the highway. North of this path stands a large, unrestored structure known as the Great Pyramid. Just before the path reaches the arch a smaller path veers off to the left and leads to three small structures. The structures are unrestored and are heavily overgrown with vegetation. They do, however, give one some idea of what archaeologists are faced with when clearing and restoring a site.

The most important structure in this section of Kabah is the arch. Unlike the arch at Labna, it is unadorned and, unlike those in Uxmal's Palace of the Governor, it was never part of a building. Nonetheless, it is a magnificent example of the Mayan Arch.

In order to reach Sayil, Xlapak and Labna it is necessary to continue south for three miles on Route 261. At this point there is a sign for Sayil which is approximately two miles farther. This road continues on beyond Xlapak and Labna but does not go to Uxmal. In order to return to Uxmal, or to go on to Campeche, it is necessary to return to Route 261.

Sayil the Easy Way

A visit to Sayil can be exhausting but it does not have to be. Visitors should keep in mind that it is hot and humid in this area and that distances between structures are great at this site. Furthermore, the Palace and El Mirador, the two most interesting structures at Sayil, can be reached easily.

Hooked Nose God

The Palace is the most beautiful and, also, the most complete structure at Sayil. Since it is only a short walk from the parking lot, it is also the easiest to reach. The Palace is a magnificent structure consisting of three stepped tiers containing numerous rooms. In

SAYIL

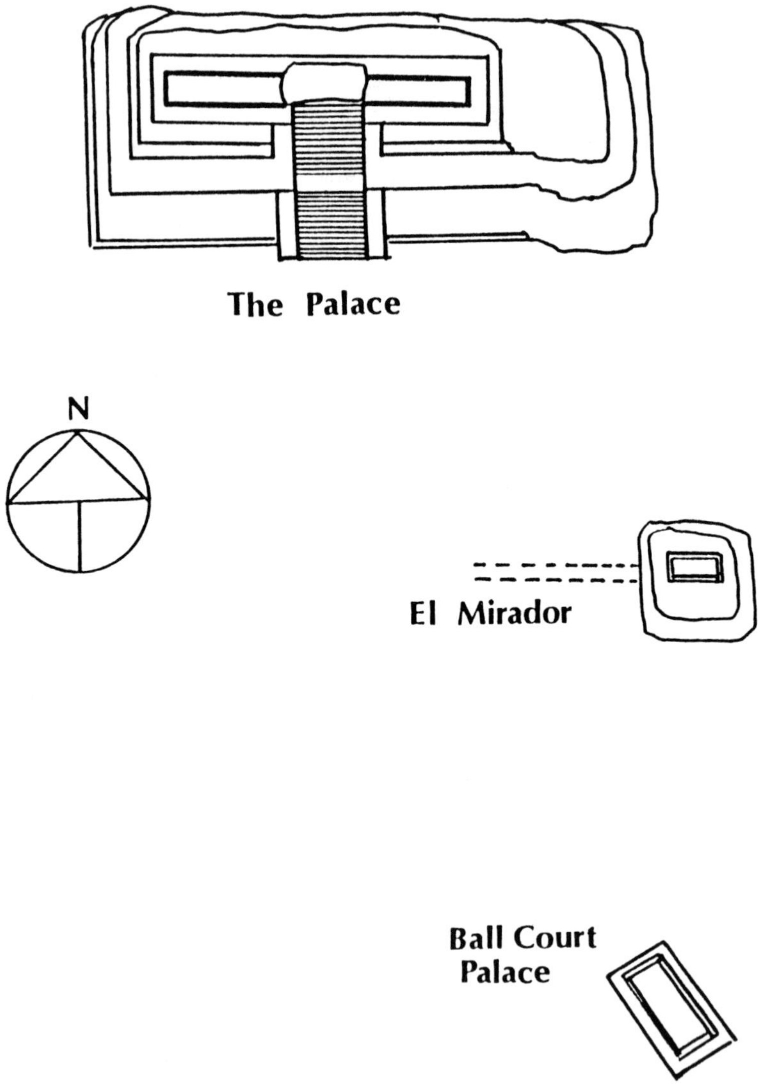

the center of the facade is an immense staircase which has not been completely restored. Of the Palace's three levels, the facade of the second level is the most highly decorated. It contains numerous columns of various sizes and many of these columns, though made of stone, are reminiscent of bamboo. Across the upper portion of this tier is a beautiful frieze whose corners bear Chaac masks with large hooked noses which protrude from the building. The rest of the frieze is made up of small columns interspersed with a large Chaac mask and representations of a divinity known both as the Diving God and the Descending God. This god takes his name from the posture of his body which resembles that of a person diving into water. Interestingly, images of this god are also found at the archaeological sites of Tulum and Coba on the eastern side of the Yucatan Peninsula.

Compared to the second story of the Palace, the first and third stories are rather plain. However, their simplicity serves to heighten the beauty of the second story.

Caught by Surprise

All three stories of the Palace are home to scores of small, harmless birds who build their nests within the many rooms. As visitors explore the Palace, it is not uncommon for the birds to swoop out and then to swoop back in. Such an occurrence may be startling but, for those who enjoy nature, it is also exhilarating. One cannot help but admire the grace, speed and agility of these creatures.

Hidden Ruin from a Special Vantage

Visitors exploring the palace should not miss climbing to the top. From this vantage point, if one stands with one's back to the central stairway, it is possible to see a panorama of the surrounding countryside and, far off on a distant hill, one can see a solitary Mayan ruin. Behind and to the west of the palace is a *chultun* which can also be seen from this vantage point.

The Phallic Carving

A short distance from the palace is an unrestored pyramid known as El Mirador, the Lookout. The rubble is surmounted by a temple with a beautiful roof comb. A short distance beyond El Mirador is a large, extremely phallic, carving of a man.

LABNA

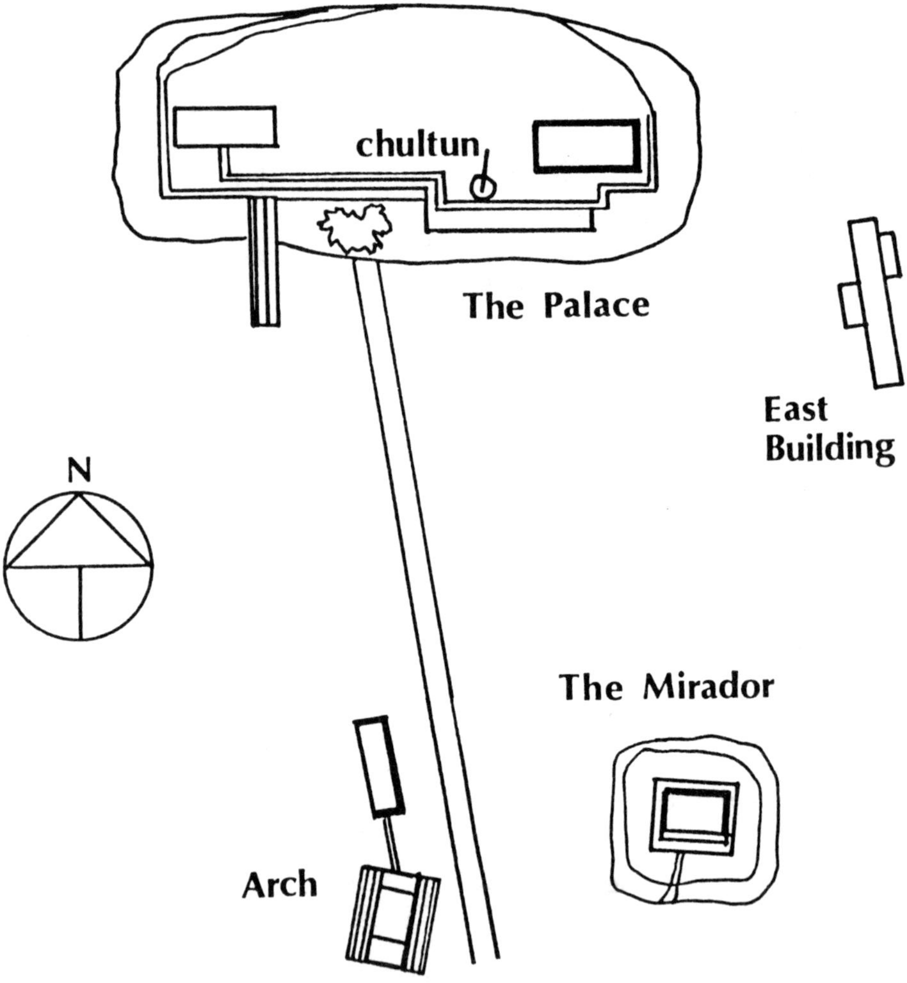

There are other structures at Sayil but they are more difficult to reach. For example, in an area termed the Ball Court, there is a structure that is reminiscent of the Palace. Although not much restoration work has been done, it is, nonetheless, beautiful. However, in order to see it, it is necessary to walk for a long distance on a narrow path through dense vegetation. The walk is made exhausting by the heat, humidity and numerous insects. Insect repellent is necessary at Sayil and it is essential if one intends to visit the ball court area or any of the other outlying areas of this site.

Visual Feast

Approximately four miles beyond Sayil lie the ruins of Xlapak. There is only one structure at this site but it is extremely beautiful. The lower part of the building is extremely plain but the upper portion is richly decorated with Chaac masks and geometric designs. The Chaac masks at the corners of the building display the typical, protruding, hooked noses which are seen at other sites in this area of the Yucatan. Although this structure is only partially restored, it is a visual feast and makes Xlapak well worth a visit.

Easy Place to Visit

Labna, another of the most beautiful and photogenic archaeological sites in the area, is only two miles past Xlapak. The main structures of this site are spread out over a large area which is kept well cleared of vegetation. This makes a visit to Labna relatively easy. The Palace, the East Building, the Arch and El Mirador comprise the major structures at Labna.

Human Head in Serpent's Mouth

The Palace is quite large and, though not entirely restored, it contains a number of interesting features. It is somewhat pyramidal in design and its most interesting characteristics are found on the first level. The lower portion of the facade of this level contains numerous columns similar to those of the Palace at Sayil. The upper portion of the facade consists of beautiful geometric designs and magnificent Chaac masks. Also at this level is a carving of a serpent with its jaws open and a human head emerging from them. This carving is similar to one known as the Queen of Uxmal which is now in the National Museum of Anthropology in Mexico City.

Other interesting aspects of the Palace area are a *chultun*, which is built into the Palace, and the remains of a *sacbe*, a Mayan ceremonial road, which begins in front of the palace and which continues in the direction of the Arch and El Mirador.

A short distance from the Palace is a structure known simply as the East Building. This structure is much smaller than the Palace but columns on its upper facade resemble those of Labna's Palace as well as those on the Palace at Sayil.

An Arch, Stone Heads and a Phallus

The most famous structure at Labna is the Arch. It is beautifully detailed on both sides and is one of the most exquisite of Maya creations. The stonework of the west facade contains Mayan huts, delicate latticework designs and a Chaac mask. (A few feet from this side of the Arch there are a few carved stone heads and a large stone phallus.) Because it is made up solely of large geometric designs, the decoration of the Arch's east facade is in sharp contrast to those of the west facade. Originally there were small structures adjacent to the Arch. Restoration work has only been done on those structures which stood north of the Arch. However, it is still possible to see how these structures were meant to visually compliment both facades of the Arch.

The Labna Arch, the Arch at Kabah and those of the Palace of the Governor at Uxmal are the classic and the most beautiful examples of the Mayan Arch. As such, they should be seen by anyone with an interest in Mayan art and architecture.

Superb Spot for Photographs

Just beyond the east side of the Arch is a structure known both as El Mirador, the Lookout, and as El Castillo, the Castle. As with El Mirador at Sayil, all that remains of what was once a pyramid is a pile of stones surmounted by a temple with a roof comb. However, from the temple one has an excellent view of the entire Palace as well as an excellent view of the Arch's east facade.

Special Opportunity

A visit to Labna, as well as to Xlapak, Sayil and Kabah, adds depth to one's understanding of Mayan achievement and affords ample opportunities to experience a wide range of Mayan architectural artistry. Such visits also afford the opportunity of seeing sites in varying stages of restoration, thereby, making the tasks and accomplishments of archaeologists more comprehensible.

Tours can be arranged to these sites but the best way to visit them is by rental car. It is best to reserve an entire day to see these four ruins. Trying to see them on the same day one visits Uxmal would not do justice to any of the sites.

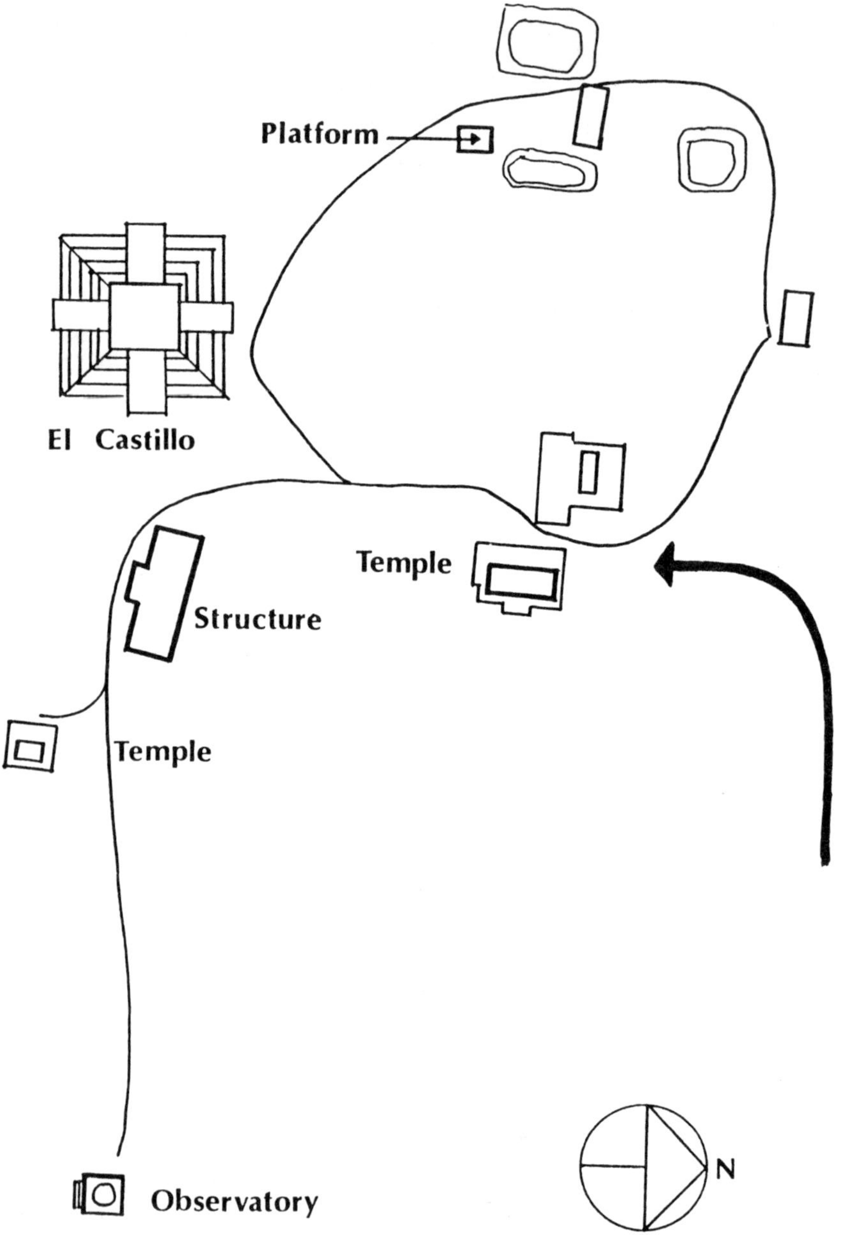
Platform
El Castillo
Temple
Structure
Temple
Observatory
N

MAYAPAN

Chapter 16

MAYAPAN

City of Violence

Little remains of the once great city of Mayapan. The few existing structures at the site offer silent testimony to the city's almost complete eradication. Mayapan has a tragic aura that is almost palpable. Even visitors to the site who are unaware of the city's fate can sense that it was purposefully destroyed, not simply abandoned.

Devastation Total

Once, over 3,000 structures stood at Mayapan, a city with a population of 10,000. The entire city was enclosed behind a protective wall and was able to control most of Northern Yucatan for well over two hundred years. Since Mayapan is in an area which is, for the most part, unsuitable for agriculture, it was necessary for the city to get its supplies, in the form of tribute, from neighboring cities. The rulers of Mayapan insured a steady flow of tribute by keeping the rulers of the tribute cities prisoner at Mayapan. Eventually, the demand for supplies became so burdensome that it precipitated a revolt. In the upheaval, Mayapan was burned. Visiting the site today, one has the impression that the intention of the insurgents was to erase all evidence of the city's existence. The total devastation is evident throughout the site.

No Human Control

The first impression visitors get of Mayapan is from an almost totally destroyed structure. At the top of this pile of rubble, the roots of a tree are entwined about stone blocks, supporting them off the ground. This sight epitomizes the fate of Mayapan: Here humans are no longer in control.

Near this mound of rubble is a small, ruined temple which has only been slightly restored. The only interesting detail remaining on the structure is a stone serpent's head on one corner of its stairway.

More Evidence of Violence

Beyond this small temple stands a pyramid known as El Castillo. Once it was, undoubtedly, among Mayapan's most impressive structures. Now it impresses because it is further evidence of the violence which, literally, tore this city apart. Thought to be modeled after El Castillo at Chichen Itza, Mayapan's pyramid is smaller and little restoration has been done on it. Lying about in the plaza in front of the pyramid are numerous architectural and sculptural fragments found at the site.

To the east of the pyramid is an overgrown natural well, known as a cenote. A few feet past the cenote are the remains of a columned structure. The most interesting aspect of this building is an extremely large mask of the god Chaac. It is similar to those that can be seen at Uxmal, Kabah, Sayil, Xlapak and Labna.

A short distance farther east is a circular structure built on a platform. Believed to be an observatory, it is similar to the one at Chichen Itza, known as El Caracol. The building at Mayapan, however, is much smaller. The observatory is Mayapan's only other remaining structure of importance.

Although, today, Mayapan is not a large site, it does offer an interesting contrast to larger and greatly restored sites such as Uxmal and Chichen Itza.

For the Adventurous

Mayapan can be reached from Uxmal and the best way to visit the site is on a return trip to Merida. However, traveling to Merida via Mayapan, as opposed to using the direct route from Uxmal, adds approximately two hours in travel time. Also, to reach Mayapan from Uxmal requires some patience. It is necessary to pass through a number of small towns where it is easy to make a wrong turn and get lost. The placement of road signs is poor to nonexistent and it is necessary to ask directions often. However, for those wishing to see something overlooked by most travelers, a visit to Mayapan may be well worth the effort.

Chapter 17

CHICHEN ITZA

Superstar of the Yucatan

Since the creation of Cancun as a resort area, Chichen Itza has become one of the most visited archaeological sites in Mexico. Located in the state of Yucatan, Chichen Itza (open 8 a.m. to 5 p.m.) is but a few hours drive from either Cancun to the east, or Merida, to the west, and day trips are possible from either area. This, however, is the least desirable way to experience Chichen Itza.

World Wonder

Because of Chichen Itza's proximity to the popular resort of Cancun, people, who otherwise would have had little or no exposure to Mayan civilization, are able to take a tour bus directly to this major site. Unfortunately, this type of visit does not leave much time to truly experience the essence of Chichen Itza. It is difficult, if not impossible, to get any sense of the sacred or profane aspects of this site after having endured a few hours on a bus only to be herded about with a horde of other travelers. Chichen Itza, like the other pre-Hispanic cities, should be quietly savored. It is a place for contemplation. This was a city of gods and humans upon which three cultures left their mark. The Maya, the Toltecs and the Itza, a Toltec clan which spoke Mayan, each contributed to what is today considered one of the world's great archaeological wonders.

Exotic Hotel

Although Chichen Itza can be visited in one day, it is best to spend at least two full days at the site. There are a number of fine hotels nearby. Among the finest is the Hotel Mayaland which is located closest to the ruins. Situated in a tropical setting, the Hotel Mayaland has a main wing plus individual bungalows built in typical Yucatecan style. The bungalows are extremely picturesque but it must be pointed out, however, that insects and other small creatures can and do get into the bungalows through the thatched roofs. For those who would be made uncomfortable by this, a stay in the main wing, built in the style of a colonial hacienda, is well

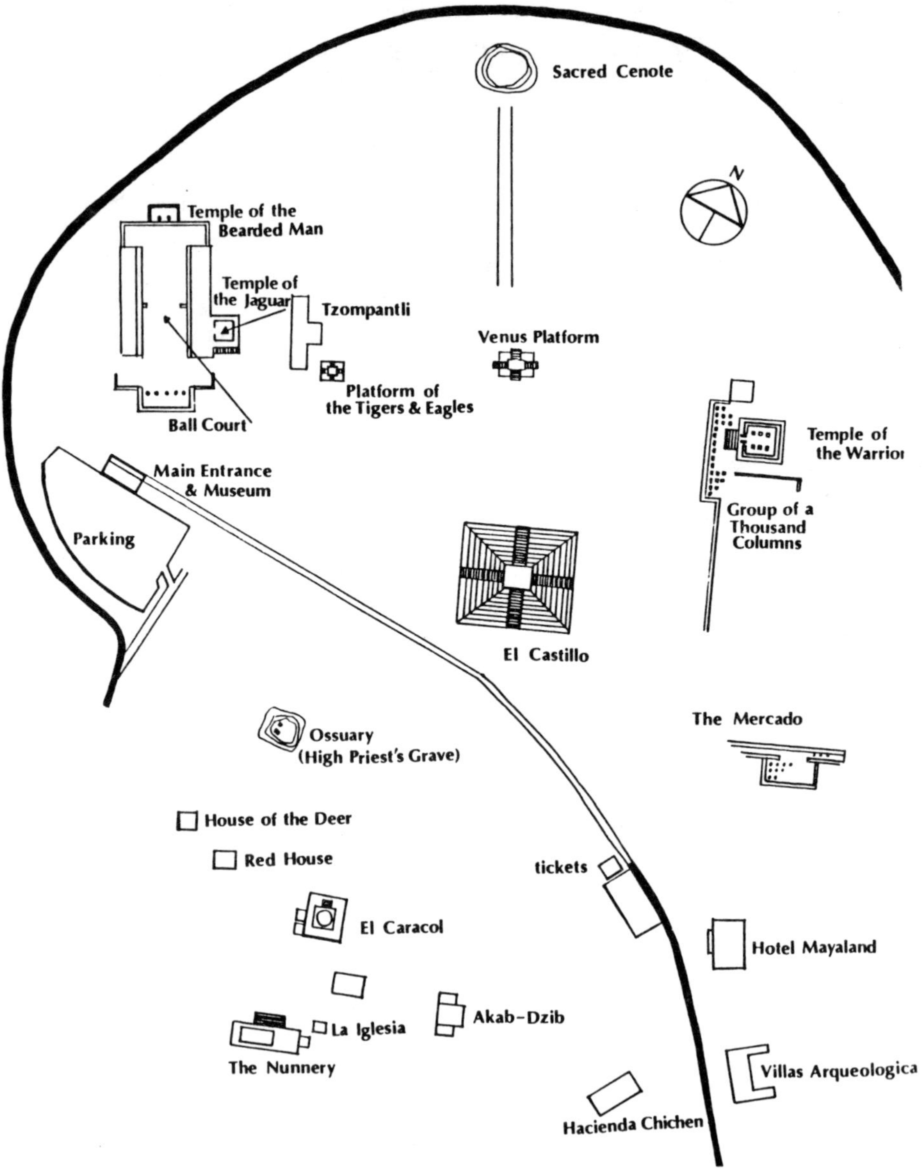

CHICHEN ITZA

recommended. Located in the main wing, the dining room is extremely pleasant. From it one has a view past bougainvillea covered archways to the pool. Around the pool are thatched umbrellas, known as *palapas*, which add to the tropical ambience of the hotel. Although the Yucatan Peninsula is arid scrubland, the grounds of the Hotel Mayaland are lush with tropical vegetation. Walkways meander through the landscape affording the opportunity for quiet, romantic strolls amid ginger, palms, banana trees and the sounds of gently splashing fountains. Besides the beauty of the hotel itself, its proximity to the ruins offers some interesting views of Chichen Itza, especially of the observatory across the highway.

There is also a Villas Arqueologicas hotel near the site which is almost identical in design to Villas Arqueologicas hotels at other major archaeological sites in Mexico. It, too, affords charm and modern comfort as well as a location conveniently near the ruins. Rooms at the Villas Arqueologicas are air conditioned and the food served at this hotel is, perhaps, the finest in the area.

Across the road is Hacienda Chichen which is also a good choice. One could not ask for a more lovely setting and it, too, is but a short distance from the ruins.

Traditionally the two sections which make up Chichen Itza have been termed "new" and "old." When the highway cut through the ruins, the section north of the road was usually designated new Chichen while the south section was termed old Chichen. These terms are a misnomer and are extremely misleading since structures in each section are from various periods.

Recently, the section of the highway that ran through the ruins was removed and this area has been beautifully landscaped with paths and trees. In addition, a visitors' center has been built which has a parking lot, a small museum, a money exchange, shops, rest rooms, a refreshment area and a miniature reconstruction of the site.

Mexico's Most Famous Pyramid

Of all the structures at Chichen Itza, the most well known is El Castillo which is in the area north of the highway. For some reason this magnificent pyramid reminded the Spanish of a castle and that is what they called it. Also known as the Temple of Kukulcan, it can be seen well above the tops of the nearby trees. Kukulcan is a direct translation into Mayan of the name Quetzalcoatl. According to legend, this great culture hero, known as the feathered serpent, came to the Yucatan Peninsula after leaving the city of Tula. According to one version of the myth, Quetzalcoatl lived for a time among the Mayas at Chichen Itza where he taught the people many wise and useful things. Finally, it is said that Quetzalcoatl sailed away on a raft of feathers but had promised to return one day. El Castillo is a stepped pyramid which is surmounted by a temple. On each side of the pyramid there is a great staircase but only two have been restored. The climb to the top is somewhat difficult and is made more so by the steepness of the stairway and by the tropical climate. From the top of El Castillo one has an excellent view of the Temple of the Warriors, the Great Ballcourt and of many other structures in the north section. Within El Castillo are the remains of an earlier structure which contains a red jaguar throne. The eyes and spots of the jaguar are of jade. The entrance to visit this earlier structure is on the ground level on the north side of the pyramid. Unfortunately, however, it is often closed.

Serpents, Eagles and Jaguars

A short distance from the west side of El Castillo is a structure known as the Platform of the Tigers and Eagles. At the top of each of the four stairways are two serpent heads and the sides of the structure are decorated with images of feathered serpents, eagles and jaguars. This platform is associated with two divisions within the Toltec warrior ranks known as the Tigers and the Eagles. In Mexico the word tiger actually refers to the jaguar.

Major Complex

Beyond the Platform of the Tigers and Eagles is the Ball Court Complex which consists of the Temple of the Jaguars, the Temple of the Bearded Man and the Ball Court itself. One of seven ball courts at Chichen Itza, this playing field is the largest at the site and it is also far larger than those at Uxmal or Palenque.

The Temple of the Jaguars is made up of a lower and an upper level. The lower level faces El Castillo and within this section of the temple is a carved stone jaguar which is similar in stance and expression to the jaguar within El Castillo. There are also many interesting carvings on this level.

Monstrous Serpents of Stone

To the left of the lower level is a flight of stone stairs which lead to the upper portion of the structure which faces the ball court playing area. On this level are two huge and magnificent columns carved in the form of serpents. These are representations of Kukulcan, the feathered serpent. At the uppermost portion of these columns one can see the enormous rattles of the serpents. Within this portion of the temple there is a fresco depicting Toltec warriors engaged in battle. If one is lucky, this section of the temple will be open and the frescoes can be viewed. For those wishing to take photographs, the upper level of the Temple of the Jaguar offers unparalleled overviews of the Ball Court and of the Temple of the Bearded Man.

Losing the Game Meant Losing One's Head

Even though little is known with any certainty about the game played at this site and throughout ancient Meso-America, the Ball Court, is nonetheless, fascinating. Two carved stone goals are in place on the walls of the two sides of the playing field. The object of the game, known as pok-ta-pok, was to hit a rubber ball through the stone hoop without using one's hands. In comparison to the modern game of basketball, the hoops are sideways making a goal more difficult to achieve. It is believed that, as in the modern game of soccer, players kept the ball in motion with head, shoulders, elbows, hips and feet. Along the walls of the ball court are bas-reliefs which clearly depict some of the more gruesome aspects of the game. It is easy, for example, to make out the decapitated head of the captain of a losing team in these reliefs.

Most Interesting Phenomenon

At the end of the ball court farthest from the Temple of the Jaguar stands the Temple of the Bearded Man which derives its name from the bas-relief within. However, what is most interesting about this small temple is the fact that a person speaking in normal tones in the temple can be heard at the far end of the Ball Court.

The Skull Rack

Just to the west of the Ball Court is another low platform similar to the Platform of the Tigers and Eagles. Known as Tzompantli or skull racks, Toltec structures such as this were made up either of human skulls or of carved skulls. This structure also contains interesting carvings of eagles, serpents and warriors.

Beyond this skull rack is a similar structure known as the Venus Platform. It was so named because of carvings on it representing the morning star, Venus. Also depicted on the platform are open-mouthed serpents which are excellent for close-up photography. Nearby are the remains of a stone Chac-Mool. Chac-Mools are reclining male figures which hold between their hands an offering bowl which rests upon their abdomen.

Well of Human Sacrifice

Near the Venus Platform is a large road known as the Sacred Causeway. This road leads to the Well of Sacrifice which is also known as the Sacred Cenote. *Cenotes* are natural wells and there are two at Chichen Itza. One was considered sacred and the other was the only source of water for the inhabitants of the city. Since water is scarce in this region such wells were of great importance. Cities, like Uxmal, which lacked *cenotes* built large cisterns to catch and hold rainwater whenever possible. The sacred well was of great importance to the inhabitants of Chichen Itza in a different way. Offerings were made here to the rain god, Chaac, who was believed to reside in the *cenote*. It was also believed that humans sacrificed at the well could carry messages to the gods. Adult males and females as well as children were sacrificed by drowning. Various objects, many of which were first ritually damaged, were also offered. Objects of gold, silver, copper, jade and amber have been dredged from the Sacred Cenote. Unfortunately, a great many of these artifacts were stolen from the National Museum of Anthropology in Mexico City on December 24, 1985.

Offerings of Human Hearts

The last major area to visit in the north section of Chichen Itza is the Temple of the Warriors. The Temple of the Warriors is a large stepped pyramid built over an earlier temple. This inner temple can be visited but the hours when it is open vary. The Temple of the Warriors takes its name from the numerous columns in front of it which are carved with magnificently detailed depictions of warriors. At the top of the structure's great staircase is the actual temple. In front of the temple are a stone Chac-Mool and two huge serpent columns similar to those of the Temple of the Jaguar. In the Chac-Mool's offering dish were placed still beating human hearts as offerings to the gods. The facade of the temple is decorated with stylized masks of the rain god, Chaac. These are easily recognized by the hooked noses which protrude from the walls and which resemble curved elephant trunks. Within the temple there are quite a number of columns carved with bas-reliefs. There are also some stone slabs supported by small carved figures, known as the Atlantean Table, because the figures resemble the far larger Atlantes of Tula. It is interesting because the figures supporting the table top are individualized.

Time should be spent exploring all four sides of the temple and of the stepped pyramid upon which it rests. These walls contain numerous stone masks as well as representations of eagles, jaguars and serpents which are excellent choices for close-up photography.

At the south end of the Warrior pyramid are numerous columns which are known as the Group of the Thousand Columns although there are far less than a thousand columns to be seen. The symmetry of these columns makes them worth a brief visit.

Nearby is a group of columns known as El Mercado because, to the Spanish, this area looked like a marketplace. It is believed that, as protection from the sun, the columns had a roof of some sort. However, no evidence of a roof has been found. Perhaps, if the colonnade was roofed, the material used was of a perishable nature. Also in the general area of the Group of the Columns and El Mercado are the remains of a steam bath and two ball courts.

Other Essential Sights

The area south of the highway contains numerous buildings and, of these, the Observatory and the Nunnery Complex should not be missed. The other structures can be visited based on the time one has available and the interest one has in archaeology.

Importance of Time

To a people obsessed with time, the observatory served an important function. The Maya placed great importance upon astronomical observation and their calculations of the movements of heavenly bodies was extremely accurate. Based on their calculations, the Maya devised the most exact calendar of any ancient civilization and incessantly recorded important dates. The Maya believed that, although earlier worlds had been created and destroyed, the present universe was created in what we would designate 3114 B.C. They dated everything from this point forward.

Chichen Itza's observatory is also known as El Caracol which means snail in Spanish. It was so named because of the circular stairway within. From the top of the observatory, El Castillo can be seen looming above the trees in the distance and many of the other structures in this section of Chichen Itza can be seen.

Although the purpose of the building known as the observatory is, for the most part, accepted, the same cannot be said of the buildings which make up the Nunnery Complex. The Nunnery Complex consists of the nunnery, the nunnery annex and the church. These structures were named by the Spanish and, over the centuries, the names have remained.

Great Area for Detail Photographs

The Nunnery is a large structure with many rooms. It has a great staircase surmounted by a temple. Perhaps this building served as a palace. From the top of the Nunnery one has a splendid view of the Church and of the Observatory.

Attached to the Nunnery is a structure known as the Nunnery Annex. The detailing of this building is magnificent. The entrance on the east side is particularly interesting since one enters through the mouth of a huge monster mask. There are other masks on the facade of this builing and they are wonderfully photogenic.

The small building near the Nunnery Annex is known as the Church though it served no such purpose. Although the Church is small and its lower facade is plain, the upper area is a riot of detail. Besides its beautiful fretwork designs, the Church also has representations of a snail, an armadillo, a crab and a turtle as well as magnificent hooked-nosed masks on its upper facade and in its roof comb. For such a small structure, the church has a wealth of interesting details.

For Those with Time

Also of some interest is a structure known as the Akab-Dzib which is only a short distance from the observatory. In Mayan, Akab-Dzib means unknown writing and the building was so named for a series of undeciphered glyphs found over an interior doorway.

Other structures which are in the southern section of Chichen Itza are the High Priest's Grave, the Red House, the Deer House and the Temple of the Wall Panels. These buildings are small but may be of interest to those with a strong interest in Mayan ruins.

For Those Who Can't Get Enough

More difficult to reach are the Date Group, the Phallic Temple, the Temple of the Little Heads, the Temple of the Four Lintels and the Temple of the Hieroglyphic Jambs. These are in areas that are overgrown with vegetation and they require a good deal of walking to reach. Whereas insect repellent is helpful in other areas of Chichen Itza, it is essential if one is venturing into the outlying areas. For the average traveler, visiting these small temples may not be worth the effort.

The more time one has at Chichen Itza the more one can explore at a leisurely pace. Even if one can only visit on a day trip, Chichen Itza should not be missed since, once seen, it is never forgotten.

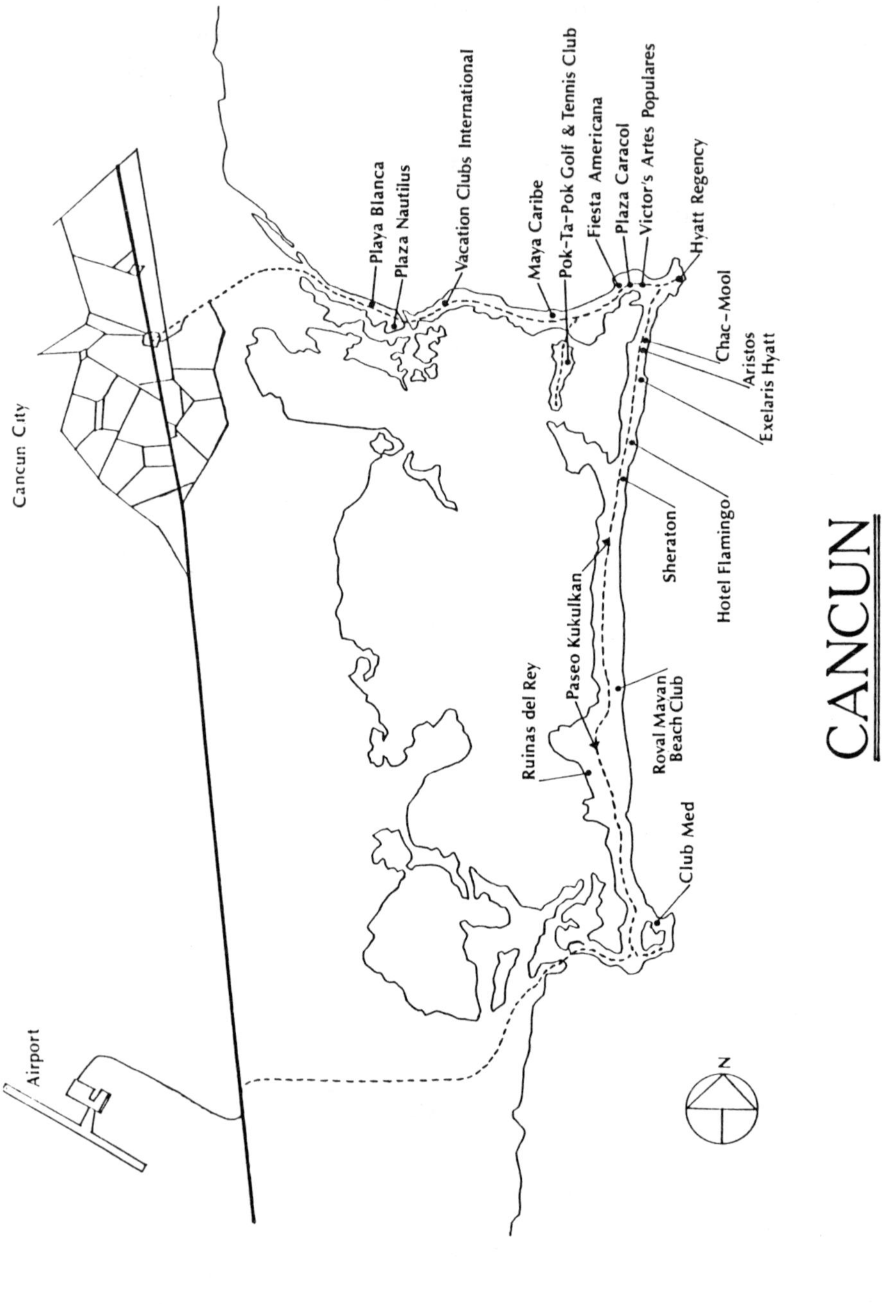
CANCUN
Cancun City
Airport
Playa Blanca
Plaza Nautilus
Vacation Clubs International
Maya Caribe
Pok-Ta-Pok Golf & Tennis Club
Fiesta Americana
Plaza Caracol
Victor's Artes Populares
Hyatt Regency
Chac-Mool
Aristos
Exelaris Hyatt
Sheraton
Hotel Flamingo
Paseo Kukulkan
Ruinas del Rey
Royal Mayan Beach Club
Club Med
N

Chapter 18

CANCUN

Most Exciting Resort in the Americas

Admittedly, Cancun is geared toward American tourists. It is commercialized, expensive and not representative of Mexico. However, it is probably what most tourists want in a resort area vacation. Cancun's water is purified, air conditioning is commonplace and English is spoken almost everywhere. This Caribbean resort has wonderful beaches, excellent hotels, fine restaurants and American-style shopping malls. Cancun also offers vacationers the opportunity to enjoy a wide range of sporting activities, as well as the opportunity to take a variety of interesting day trips. Although Cancun has little of the true flavor of Mexico, it cannot be denied that, as a resort, it succeeds admirably. Over the years, Cancun, has burgeoned from a small fishing village into a world class resort having all the amenities and diversions anyone could possibly desire.

Past, Present, Future

Cancun is an island located alongside the state of Quintana Roo on the Yucatan Peninsula. The island and the mainland are connected by means of two causeways. Less than twenty years ago, Cancun was covered by vegetation and inhabited by approximately one hundred Mayans. The Mexican Government, by computer, chose this small island as the ideal location for a new and luxurious international resort. Cancun's development is continuing and is to be completed by the year 2000.

All of Cancun's luxury hotels are on the island which is the main tourist area. Banks, government offices and less expensive hotels and restaurants are found in Cancun City, on the mainland. This city is where most of the hotel workers live.

Besides the luxury hotels, the many restaurants and the shopping malls, full ownership and time share condominiums are beginning to cover Cancun's once desolate dunes. It is hoped that the island will not be overdeveloped.

Uncrowded Beaches

Despite the great amount of buildings being erected, Cancun's beaches are, surprisingly, not overcrowded and they are magnificent. These beaches are clean; the sand is white; the water is warm and the color of turquoise. Some of the beaches have a mild surf while at others the waves are large. In Cancun, there seems to be a beach to suit everyone.

However, one of the major reasons for Cancun's popularity is that it offers vacationers more to enjoy than just lying on a beach.

Entertainment Variety

Even the many different types of hotels in Cancun can provide enjoyment. Some, like the Sheraton, offer so many activities that it would be possible to spend an entire vacation without ever having to leave the hotel's grounds. Others, like the Aristos, are luxurious but function on a smaller scale. Furthermore, most of Cancun's hotels offer some kind of free entertainment.

Cancun's Most Romantic Restaurant

Cancun also has an incredible number of restaurants serving an assortment of cuisines. One of the finest restaurants in Cancun is Chac-Mool which offers a most exceptional dining experience. Chac-Mool overlooks the Caribbean Sea, and classical music and candlelight set the mood for romance. Among the memorable dishes are lobster in cognac sauce, shrimps Pancho Villa and shrimps San Francisco.

Cure for Homesickness

Directly in front of Chac-Mool is an establishment called Mak Burger. For vacationers who are homesick for American fast foods, Mak Burger serves hamburgers, french fries and malteds as well as some Mexican foods.

Shopper's Paradise

Vacationers who enjoy shopping in American-style malls will find quite a few in Cancun. These shopping centers offer an enormous amount of goods and, because they are air conditioned, provide a cool respite from the heat. Those interested in Mexican arts and crafts should visit Victor, for *artes populares*, in the El Parian Mall. This shop, whose main branch is in Mexico City, is the best place in Cancun to purchase fine quality handicrafts and rare objects. Oddly enough, some wonderful painted, wooden animals from Oaxaca can be found in Explora, a clothing store, in the Plaza Caracol shopping mall, and at El Tianguis at the Hotel Sheraton.

Spectacular Sports

Those who prefer sports to shopping will find that numerous activities are available in Cancun. Scuba diving, deep sea fishing, snorkeling, windsurfing, sailing and water skiing are just some of the water sports which can be enjoyed on a Cancun vacation. Sports enthusiasts can also try jet skiing, para-sailing or flying over Cancun in an ultra-lite which resembles a hang glider with a rear propeller and a set of pontoons. In addition, many of Cancun's hotels have tennis courts and those wishing to play golf can do so at the eighteen hole Pok-Ta-Pok Golf Course.

A Word to the Wise

Increasingly, there are salespeople who ply the area of the Hotel Zone with the sole purpose of steering tourists into restaurants and condominium developments. These salespeople can be persistent. If you are not interested, say "No, gracias" firmly, keep walking, and repeat the phrase as many times as necessary. Also, be aware, if you buy goods from beach vendors, the quality of their merchandise cannot be guaranteed.

Most Popular Day Trips

Because of Cancun's location, vacation activities need not be confined to the resort area. Trips can be arranged to the nearby islands of Isla Mujeres, Cozumel, Contoy Island, a bird sanctuary, and to a number of archaeological sites. Tulum and Chichen Itza are the most frequently visited archaeological zones but, with a rental car, a visit to Coba is also possible. Smaller ruins can also be visited on Cancun Island. The small ruin of Yamil Lu'um overlooks the sea next to the Sheraton Hotel and the larger El Rey ruins are located between the Sheraton and Club Med. The El Rey ruins can be reached by public transportation, taxi or rental car. These ruins have been cleared of excess vegetation and are a pleasure to visit.

Little Known Beaches

Having a rental car also makes it easy to visit other swimming areas along the coast such as Xcaret, Paamul, Akumal, Chemuyil and Xel-ha lagoon which is usually combined with a visit to the ruins of Tulum.

Despite the criticisms some level against Cancun, it is a wonderful travel destination. Its beaches are glorious and vacationers are afforded a wide range of enjoyable, interesting and relaxing activities.

Chapter 19

XEL-HA

Snorkeling and Neon Fish

Of the many day trips possible from Cancun, Xel-ha is the most delightful and relaxing. This national park is a large lagoon teeming with a wide variety of tropical fish. The water is warm, it is never over ten feet deep and there are no waves. This makes Xel-ha the perfect spot for snorkeling. Even those who have never snorkeled before will have no trouble doing so at Xel-ha. The fish are friendly and most stay close to the rocks which are in the shallow water. Some of these underwater creatures are so vibrant with color they almost seem to glow.

Extra Special Tip

Showers and changing facilities are available at Xel-ha and those who wish to see the fish close up can rent snorkeling equipment. However, since the snorkeling gear is not sterilized after each use, it is a good idea to bring along some rubbing alcohol to pour over the mouthpiece to disinfect it. This affords some measure of protection.

From Cancun, Xel-ha can be reached in approximately one hour and fifteen minutes. The trip is best made by rental car or tour bus.

From Xel-ha it is ten minutes' driving time to Tulum.

Chapter 20

TULUM

Turquoise Waters and White Walled Ruins

Because Tulum is only a one hour and twenty-five minute drive from Cancun, it is one of the most visited archaeological sites in all of Mexico. It is estimated that over 4,000 people visit Tulum each day. The site is also very popular with tourists because the vegetation is kept so well manicured that it is very easy to explore Tulum's structures. Tulum is open 8 a.m. to 5 p.m. daily.

Tulum is a walled city which overlooks the Caribbean Sea. Built when the Mayan civilization was in decline, the architecture of Tulum is greatly inferior to that of Chichen Itza or Uxmal, for example. What makes Tulum spectacular is its location, not its architecture.

Two for One

Because it is only a ten minute drive from Xel-ha, most travelers visit Tulum and Xel-ha on the same day. Since Tulum's major structures face west, it is best to visit it during the afternoon hours. At this time the buildings are more easily photographed.

Although there are structures outside Tulum's wall, they are not cleared of vegetation and are difficult to reach. Furthermore, all the major buildings of this site are within the wall.

Park-Like Conditions

The numerous structures at Tulum vary in importance and in their state of preservation. Because of the park-like conditions of this site, one can easily walk around and visit as many structures as one wishes. However, the major buildings at Tulum are El Castillo, the Temple of the Descending God, the Temple of the Frescoes, structures 21 and 25, and of course, the wall.

El Castillo is the largest building at Tulum. It is a broad structure with a central stairway leading to a temple. Remains of serpent columns on this temple are similar to those of the Temple of the Jaguars and the Temple of the Warriors at Chichen Itza. This

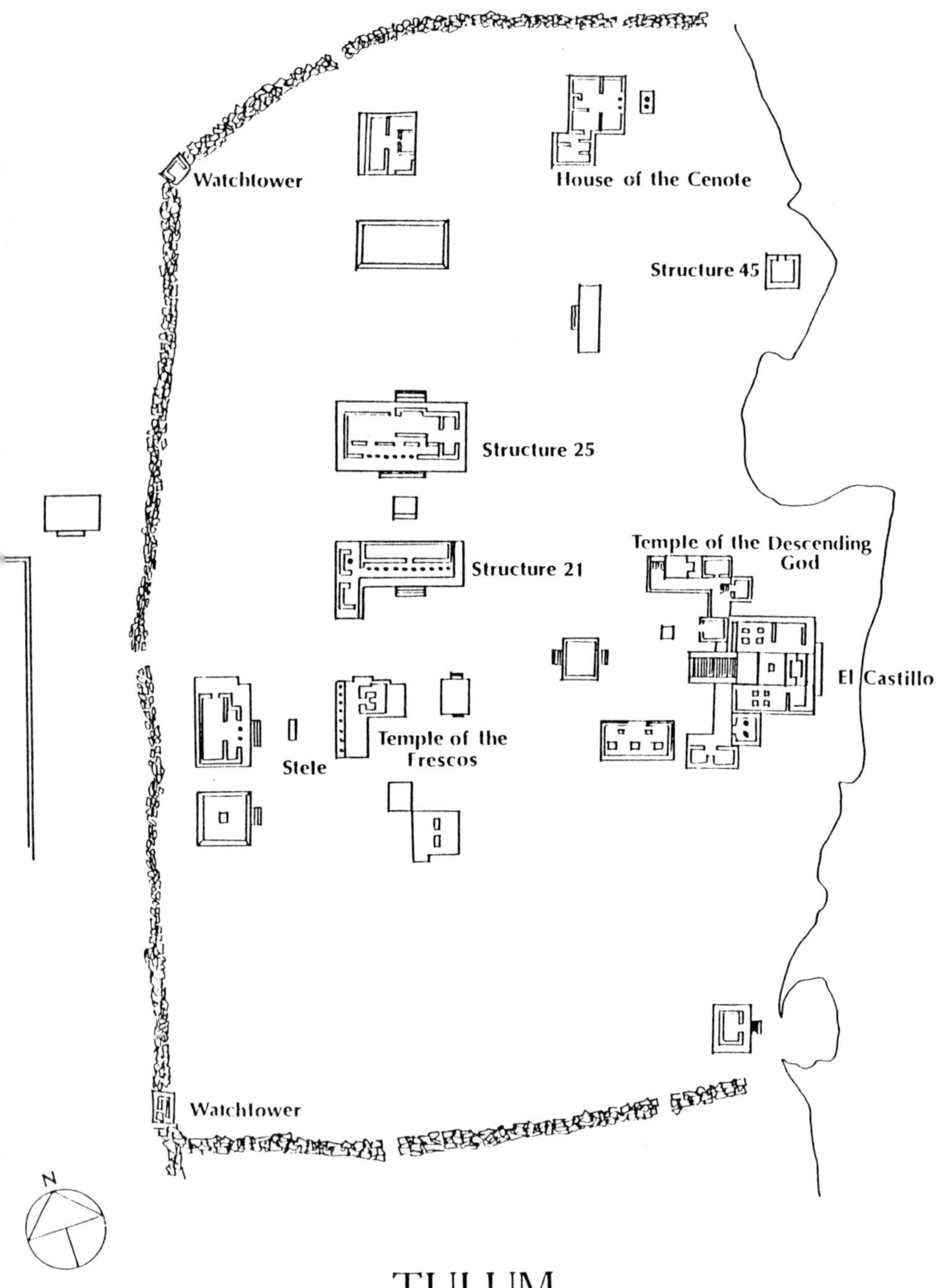
Watchtower
House of the Cenote
Structure 45
Structure 25
Structure 21
Temple of the Descending God
El Castillo
Stele
Temple of the Frescos
Watchtower
N

TULUM

temple also bears an image of the Descending God.

Unknown God

The Temple of the Descending God stands only a few feet from El Castillo. This structure is smaller than El Castillo but, it too, has a central stairway leading to a temple. Above the temple's doorways are images of the Descending God which give the temple its name. Whether this god is descending or diving remains a matter of opinion. Since the figure has what apears to be wings, it may represent a bee god. In ancient times beekeeping was an important part of life in the Yucatan since the Maya used honey with many foods. Even among the modern Maya of the Yucatan, honey is extremely important. However, it has also been postulated that the figure represents the setting sun, not a bee god, and that the wings represent the sun's rays. Whoever this god was may forever remain a mystery. However, it is clear that he was very important to the people of Tulum since his image is found on numerous structures throughout the city. Images of this god are also found inland at Coba and, on the opposite side of the Yucatan Peninsula, at Sayil.

For many visitors to Tulum, the Temple of the Frescoes is more interesting than either El Castillo or Temple of the Descending God. This structure consists of a small temple resting upon a somewhat larger structure. There is no longer any access to the upper level but almost all of the interesting details of the Temple of the Frescoes are on the lower level.

Optical Illusion

The Descending God is represented on the lower level and the northwest and southwest corners of this level consist of huge faces bearing remnants of their original paint. Though in plain view, these large faces are often missed by visitors since they are incorporated into the architecture and have the quality of an optical illusion.

Hints of Former Glory

On the west facade of this section of the building red handprints are visible. From this area it is easy to view the frescoes for which this structure is named. The wall paintings have deteriorated and parts are missing. They are, nonetheless, quite beautiful. Mayan gods, glyphs, designs, and even fish appear in the frescoes. These paintings also give some idea of how the rest of Tulum once looked. Originally all of Tulum's buildings were covered with numerous layers of stucco and were decorated with bright colors. Unfortunately, for the modern visitor, the paintings in the Temple of the Frescoes only hint at Tulum's former beauty.

Structures 21 and 25 are a short distance from the Temple of the Frescoes and each has an interesting feature. Structure 21 is noted for X-shaped designs in its windows and structure 25 is noted for its intricate stucco representation of the Descending God.

Most Important Feature

The most important feature of Tulum is not any of its buildings. The wall which surrounds the city on three sides was essential for the protection it afforded. The area of the city which faced the sea did not need a wall since it was protected by high cliffs. Today, the wall and its watchtowers are, for the most part, intact. From the top of El Castillo one has an overview of this wall which surrounds Tulum.

For many, Tulum is their introduction to Mexico's archaeological wonders. After having visited this beautiful site, such visitors are usually curious enough to want to see more of Mexico's fabled ruins.

Chapter 21

COBA

Jungle Adventure

Of all the accessible archaeological sites in Mexico, Coba is one of the most difficult to explore. For the most part, Coba is unrestored. The jungle is dense and the structures are far apart. Even early in the morning, it is hot and humid at Coba. If the jungle did not form a canopy over the paths, the heat and humidity would be unbearable.

Coba, which is open from 8 a.m. to 5 p.m., is a huge site but there are only three main areas that should be visited: the Grupo Coba, the Conjunto las Pinturas and the Nohoch Mul pyramid.

The Grupo Coba is a large pyramid with an adjoining structure. This area is the closest to the parking lot and is, therefore, easy to reach. The pyramid is only partially restored but it is, nonetheless, impressive for its size and mass. From the top of the pyramid one can see across the jungle to Lake Coba.

Farther into the jungle is a structure known as the Conjunto las Pinturas. This small pyramid has a temple at its summit which contains the remains of some frescoes. The structure takes its name from these paintings.

High Above the Jungle

The largest structure at Coba is the Nohoch Mul pyramid which is reached by means of a long path through the jungle. In the area of the pyramid there is a well preserved Mayan stele. Glyphs and five figures can be seen clearly on it.

At the top of the Nohoch Mul's one hundred and twenty steps there is a temple bearing images of the god known as the Diving or Descending God.

The heat and humidity make a climb to the top of the Nohoch Mul pyramid exhausting. However, from the top one has a panoramic view over the jungle canopy and it is possible to see a large, unrestored mound which rises above the trees.

For Those with Adventure in Their Souls

At Coba one may see snakes, frogs, lizards and large crawling

COBA

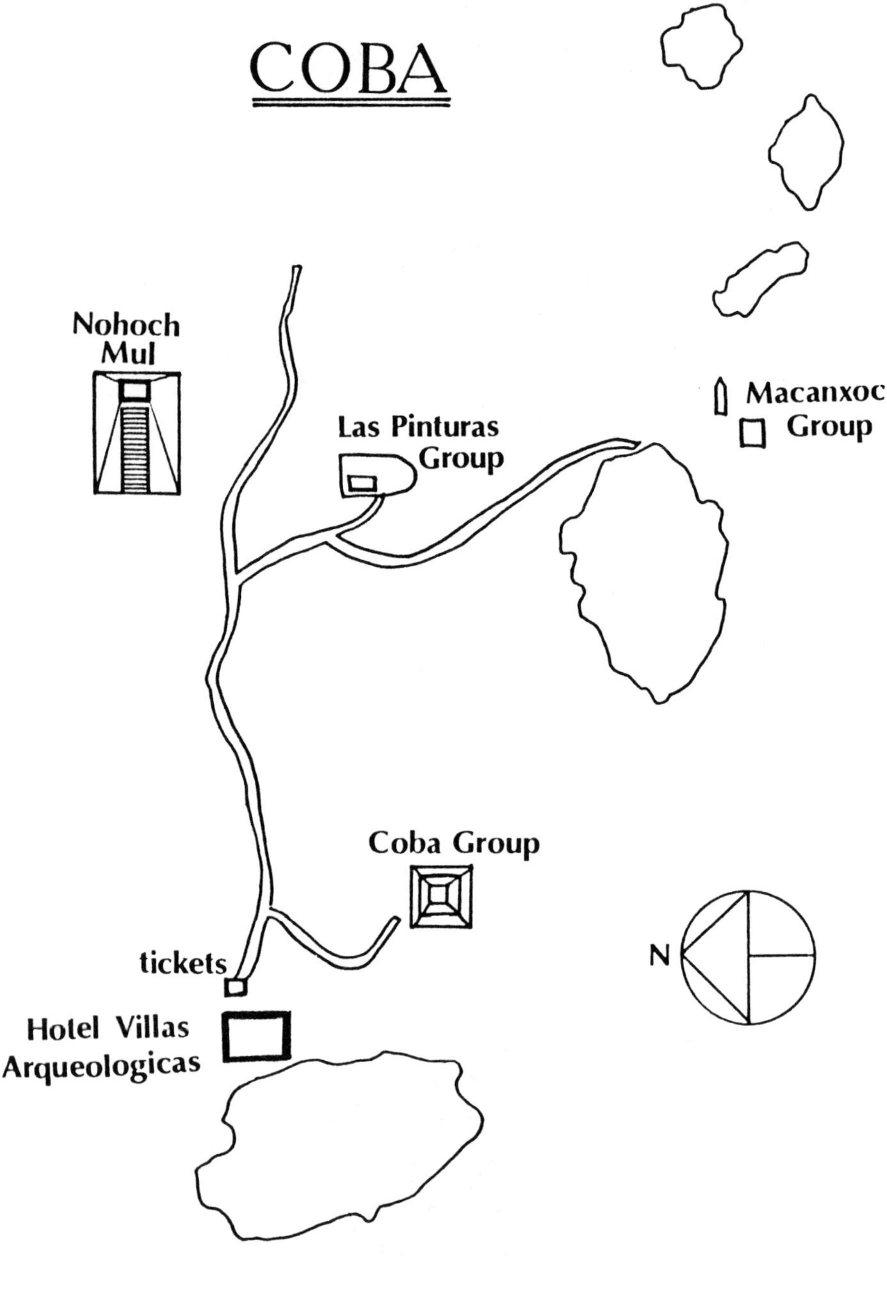
Nohoch
Mul
Las Pinturas
Group
Macanxoc
Group
Coba Group
N
tickets
Hotel Villas
Arqueologicas

insects. Because of the many flying insects, repellent is essential. This is not a place for the squeamish. The jungle is dense and, for many people, it quickly becomes oppressive. This site is a far cry from the manicured grounds of Tulum and this should be kept in mind by those considering a visit to Coba. However, for the adventurous, Coba affords the opportunity to experience what an archaeological site is like before it is cleared and restored.

A Place to Pamper Oneself

Fortunately, if one does decide to visit Coba and exploring it becomes overwhelming, one can always retreat to the comfort of the nearby Villas Arqueologicas hotel to relax. This beautiful hotel is virtually identical to the Villas Arqueologicas at other archaeological sites in Mexico and its amenities are certainly needed after a few hours of exploring the Coba ruins.

Extra Special Tips

Airport Taxes

Leave extra money for departure taxes. A small tax must be paid at the airport on all national and international flights.

Altitude

At higher altitudes, such as in Mexico City, be sure to go slowly for the first few days. Eat lightly, especially at night, and avoid alcohol.

Cameras and Film

Bring extra batteries and sufficient film.

Crime Prevention

The crime rate in Mexico, as compared to most other countries, is low. In general, tourists need not fear violent crime. As elsewhere, however, it is wise to guard against theft. Always be aware of your personal belongings. Hold on to cameras and handbags; do not let them carelessly dangle from your shoulder by their straps. Never leave valuables in a car—this includes the trunk.

Driving

Never drive at night because roads are unlighted. There may be people or animals in the road or you may hit pot-holes or *topes* (speed bumps). In Mexico City, use public transportation or taxis. Before getting into a taxi, ask the price of the trip, and then bargain. However, you can only bargain before you get into the taxi.

Electricity

Electrical current in Mexico is now the same as that used in the United States.

Entry Requirements

No inoculations are required. However, see your doctor for recommendations. A tourist card is required for entry into Mexico. You can get this card from your travel agent, your airline or from a Mexican consulate. Proof of citizenship is also required. The best form of proof is a valid passport. It will also make cashing travelers' checks easier.

Food

Mexican food is not fiery hot. Spicy hot sauces are served on the side. Do try *sopa de lima* (a Yucatecan soup made with chicken and limes), *sopa de tortilla* (tortilla soup), *sopa de aguacate fria* (cold cream of avocado soup), *huachinango a la Veracruzana* (red snapper with tomatoes, chiles, olives, onions and capers), *mole poblano* (chicken in a chocolate sauce which does not taste like chocolate), and *camarones en pipian verde* (shrimp in green pumpkinseed sauce).

Gasoline

Keep your tank full. Never let it go below half, since gas may be hard to get. In some areas, gas stations are few and far between. When getting gas make sure the pump meter has been turned back to zero, and that all the gas goes into the tank, not on the ground.

Health Precautions

To avoid stomach upsets observe the following precautions. Don't overtax yourself. Drink only bottled water. Have all drinks without ice *(sin hielo)*. Drink alcohol in moderation. Drink mineral water and carbonated beverages to replace fluids. Wash your hands before eating. Eat in moderation and avoid greasy foods. Eat only cooked vegetables. Eat only fruits which can be peeled and whose skin has not been punctured. Do not eat salads. Never eat foods sold by street vendors. Rinse your toothbrush and your mouth with bottled water. Shower with your mouth closed. Avoid overexposure to the sun.

Illegal Drugs

Mexican authorities do not take kindly to the use of illegal drugs. Anyone caught using them will find him(her)self in jail.

Language

Spanish is the national language of Mexico. In many areas, Indian languages are spoken as well. It is not necessary to speak Spanish, but knowing a few essential phrases is helpful.

Maps

It is a good idea to bring road maps with you. However, they can usually be purchased in book stores.

Money

Exchange money in banks or at your hotel. Do not exchange money with persons who may approach you on the street. Use travelers' checks, but also bring a small amount of U.S. dollar bills.

Museums

In general, museums are closed on Monday. Take this into consideration when planning your itinerary.

Novels

The following novels afford good reading on Mexico: ***Aztec*** by Peter Jennings (Avon); ***The Luck of Huemac*** by Daniel Peters (Random House).

Numbers to Know

Those wishing up-to-the-minute health and travel advisories can call the State Department Overseas Citizen's Emergency Center in Washington, DC at (202) 647-5225, Monday through Friday 8:15 a.m. to 10 p.m. and on Saturday 9 a.m. to 3 p.m. (Eastern Standard Time).

For emergencies dial: (202) 634-3600 after hours, Sunday and on federal holidays and ask for the Overseas Citizens' Services Duty Officer. The Emergency Center can give some health information but is mainly concerned with travel in terms of security for Americans.

For specific questions concerning health, consult the U.S. Public Health Service in your area. The Citizens' Emergency Center publishes a pamphlet entitled "Tips for Travelers to Mexico," which, among other things, gives advice on driving through Mexico. A copy of this pamphlet can be obtained by writing to the Public Affairs Office, Bureau of Consular Affairs, U.S. Department of State, Washington, DC 20520.

In the unlikely event that you have any problems while in Mexico, the Secretaria de Turismo has an emergency hotline number which can be called collect 24 hours a day from anywhere in Mexico or the U.S. In Mexico City call: 250-0123, 250-0493, 250-0151 or 250-0589. Outside the capital, ask for operator assistance. When calling from the U.S., first dial 01-525 and then the number.

Prescription Drugs

Bring a sufficient supply of prescription drugs you may need while traveling. Keep them in their proper containers to avoid problems.

Rental Cars

Rental cars are most readily available in the heavily-touristed areas. In less frequented places they may be difficult to obtain. Also, in the less-touristed areas cars with automatic transmission are usually not available even when requested in advance. However, it is often far less expensive and simpler to hire a car with driver. A car with driver is most desirable when making day trips from cities. Having a rental car would be preferable for longer trips.

Travel Agents

Finding a good travel agent is importrant. Have a good idea of where you want to go and what you want to see before going to an agent. Make sure the travel agent you choose has knowledge of the areas to which you plan to travel. A good travel agent is one that you can trust to give you well-informed and honest opinions.

Vouchers

It is a good idea to ask your travel agent to make duplicates of vouchers for hotels, etc. In the event that vouchers are lost after they are turned in, you will have proof of payment.

What Shoppers Need

To get pottery and other items home safely, it is a good idea to pack some bubble wrap, string, cellophane tape, masking tape, and tote bags.

A portable handle is a useful item to bring with you to Mexico, particularly if you buy a large boxed item which is tied with string.

Essential Spanish

Spanish	English
Por favor (por-fah-**vor**)	Please
Gracias (**grah**-see-ahis)	Thank you
De nada (day-**nah**-dah)	You're welcome
Buenos dias (**bway**-nohz **dee**-ahs)	Good day
Buenas tardes (**bway**-nahz **tar**-days)	Good afternoon
Buenas noches (**bway**-nahz **no**-chaze)	Good evening, good night
Si (**see**)	Yes
No (**no**)	No
Con permiso (cone pear-**me**-so)	Excuse me
Habla usted Ingles? (**ahb**-la **oo**-sted een **glayz**)	Do you speak English?
Donde esta _____ ? (dohn-day es-**tah**)	Where is __________________?
Donde esta el baño? (. . .el **bahn**-yo?)	Where is the bathroom?
Cuanto cuesta? (**kwan**-toe **kwes**-tah)	How much does it cost?
Tiene usted ________? (tee-**any** oo-**sted**)	Do you have ________________?
Agua mineral (**ah**-gwah min-ear-**al**)	Mineral water
Sin gas (**seen** gahz)	Without carbonation
Con gas (**cone** gahz)	With carbonation
Agua purificada (**ah**-gwah poo-ree-fee-**cah**-dah)	Purified water
Sin hielo (**seen** ee-**yay**-lo)	Without ice

Essential Numbers

(1)	uno (**oo**-no)	one
(2)	dos (**dose**)	two
(3)	tres (trays)	three
(4)	cuatro (**kwat**-ro)	four
(5)	cinco (**sink**-o)	five
(6)	seis (**say**-ees)	six
(7)	siete (see-**eh**-tay)	seven
(8)	ocho (**o**-cho)	eight
(9)	nueve (noo-**eh**-vay)	nine
(10)	diez (dee-**ez**)	ten
(11)	once (**own**-say)	eleven
(12)	doce (**do**-say)	twelve
(13)	trece (**tray**-say)	thirteen
(14)	catorce (**cator**-say)	fourteen
(15)	quince (**keen**-say)	fifteen
(16)	diez y seis (dee-**ez** E-**say**-ees)	sixteen
(17)	diez y siete (. . .E-see-**eh**-tay)	seventeen
(18)	diez y ocho (. . .E-**o**-cho)	eighteen
(19)	diez y nueve (. . .E-noo-**eh**-vay)	nineteen
(20)	veinte (**vayeen**-tay)	twenty
(30)	treinta (**train**-tah)	thirty
(40)	cuarenta (kwar-**en**-tah)	forty
(50)	cincuenta (sink-**went**-tah)	fifty
(60)	sesenta (say-**sen**-tah)	sixty
(70)	setenta (say-**ten**-tah)	seventy
(80)	ochenta (o-**chen**-tah)	eighty
(90)	noventa (no-**ven**-tah)	ninety
(100)	ciento, cien (see-**en**-toe)	one hundred
(500)	quinientos (keen-E-**en**-toes)	five hundred
(1000)	mil (**meal**)	one thousand

Going The Distance

(Distances are approximate)

(m = miles   km = kilometers)

From Mexico City

Long Trips:

to Puebla	85 m/ 136 km
to Cholula	78 m/126 km
to El Tajin	183 m/295 km
to Oaxaca	316 m/508 km
to Villahermosa	554 m/891 km
to Campeche	764 m/1231 km
to Merida	945 m/1520 km

Day Trips:

to Teotihuacan	32 m/ 51 km
to Tula	57 m/91 km
to Tenayuca	7 m/4.4 km
to Sta. Cecelia Acatitlan	9 m/15 km
Tenayuca to Sta. Cecelia	2 m/3 km
Sta. Cecelia to Tula	48 m/77 km

To the El Tajin ruins

Veracruz to El Tajin	120 m/180 km
Papantla to El Tajin	8.5 m/14 km

From Oaxaca City

to Ocotlan	20 m/32 km
to Teotitlan del Valle	14 m/23 km
to San Bartolo Coyotepec	7 m/12 km
to Monte Alban	5 m/10 km
to Dainzu	13 m/23 km
to Lambityeco	18 m/29 km
to Yagul	20 m/33 km
to Mitla	27 m/41 km

Other Distances

Mitla to Yagul	7 m/12 km
Yagul to Lambityeco	2 m/3 km
Lambityeco to Dainzu	5 m/10 km

To Palenque

Villahermosa to Palenque .... 95 m/59 km

Yucatan

Campeche to Etzna .... 41 m/65 km
Campeche to Merida (via MEX 261) ...... 152 m/245 km
Merida to Uxmal .... 58 m/93 km
Uxmal to Kabah .... 14 m/22 km
Kabah to Sayil ....5 m/9 km
Sayil to Xlapak ....4 m/7 km
Xlapak to Labna ....2 m/4 km
Uxmal to Mayapan .... 66 m/108 km
Mayapan to Merida .... 30 m/48 km
Merida to Chichen Itza .... 75 m/121 km
Cancun to Chichen Itza .... 125 m/202 km
Cancun to Xel-ha .... 72 m/116 km
Xel-ha to Tulum .... 8 m/13 km
Cancun to Tulum .... 80 m/129 km
Tulum to Coba .... 30 m/48 km
Cancun to coba .... 110 m/178 km

Sample flying times between selected cities within Mexico. (Flying times are approximate and are for non-stop flights.)

Mexico City to Oaxaca .... 50 min.
Mexico City to Villahermosa ....1 hr. 10 min.
Mexico City to Campeche ....1 hr. 25 min.
Mexico City to Merida ....1 hr. 25 min.
Mexico City to Cancun ....1 hr. 50 min.
Oaxaca to Villahermosa ....1 hr. 20 min.
Villahermosa to Merida .... 50 min.
Villahermosa to Cancun ....1 hr. 10 min.
Merida to Cancun .... 40 min.

A Checklist of Things To Take

____ Passport
____ Tourist card
____ Airline tickets
____ Hotel vouchers and duplicates
____ Luggage keys
____ Travelers' checks
____ Dollar bills
____ Passport number written on a separate piece of paper
____ Name and address put inside luggage
____ Prescription medicines
____ Prescription eyeglasses
____ Extra pair of prescription eyeglasses
____ Prescription for eyeglasses
____ Sunglasses
____ Eyeglass repair kit
____ Film
____ Extra batteries
____ Camera and lenses
____ Sun screens/sun tan lotion
____ Insect repellent
____ Pepto-Bismol/Lomotil/paregoric/Kaopectate
____ Band-Aids
____ Handi-Wipes
____ Dramamine
____ Small sewing kit
____ Cellophane tape
____ Masking tape
____ String
____ Bubble wrap
____ Tote bags
____ Extra shoelaces
____ Folding umbrella
____ Tissues
____ Cosmetics
____ Deodorant
____ Aspirin, throat lozenges, etc.
____ Small flashlight for interiors of ruins
____ Tweezers
____ Small scissors
____ Nail clippers
____ Ballpoint pens

ORDER BLANK

Golden West Publishers

4113 N. Longview Ave. • Phoenix, AZ 85014

Please ship the following books:

_____ **Arizona Adventure ($5.00)**
_____ **Arizona Cook Book ($3.50)**
_____ **Arizona Hideaways ($4.50)**
_____ **Arizona—Off the Beaten Path ($4.50)**
_____ **Arizona Outdoor Guide ($5.00)**
_____ **Bill Williams Mountain Men ($5.00)**
_____ **California Favorites Cook Book ($3.50)**
_____ **Chili-Lovers' Cook Book ($3.50)**
_____ **Citrus Recipes ($3.50)**
_____ **Cowboy Slang ($5.00)**
_____ **Cowboy Country Cartoons ($4.50)**
_____ **Easy Recipes for the Traveling Cook ($5.00)**
_____ **Easy Recipes for Wild Game ($6.50)**
_____ **Explore Arizona ($5.00)**
_____ **Fools' Gold ($5.00)**
_____ **Ghost Towns in Arizona ($4.50)**
_____ **Ginger Hutton...from the Heart ($5.00)**
_____ **How to Succeed Selling Real Estate ($3.50)**
_____ **In Old Arizona ($5.00)**
_____ **Mexican Desserts ($6.50)**
_____ **Mexican Family Favorites Cook Book ($5.00)**
_____ **The Other Mexico ($9.00)**
_____ **On the Arizona Road ($5.00)**
_____ **Pecan-Lovers' Cook Book ($5.00)**
_____ **Prehistoric Arizona ($5.00)**
_____ **Southwest Saga ($5.00)**
_____ **Sphinx Ranch Date Recipes ($5.00)**

Enclosed is $ ______________ (including $1 per book for postage & handling)

____
(NAME)

____
(ADDRESS)

____
(CITY) **(STATE)** **(ZIP)**

This order blank may be photo-copied.

Send long, stamped, self-addressed envelope for catalog.

Books from Golden West Publishers

Southwest Saga—the way it really was, by Southwest historian-journalist William C. McGaw—Esteban's life among the Zuni, Pancho Villa's raid north of the border, Mark Twain's drug scheme, the strange death of Ambrose Bierce, etc. (160 pages)...***$5.00***

The American cowboy had a way with words! Lingo of the American West, captured in 2000 phrases and expressions—colorful, humorous, earthy, raunchy! Includes horse and cattle terms, rodeo talk, barb wire names, cattle brands. ***Cowboy Slang*** by "Frosty" Potter, illustrated by Ron Scofield (128 pages)...***$5.00***

Dr. Snyder explains the how and why of prehistoric events. He guides you to the ruins of ancient civilizations in Arizona and their artifacts. Complete with photographs, maps, charts and index. ***Prehistoric Arizona*** by Ernest E. Snyder (128 pages)...***$5.00***

More than 250 easy-to-follow homestyle favorite family recipes for tacos, tamales, menudo, enchiladas, burros, salsas, frijoles, chile relleno, carne seca, guacamole and sweet treats! ***Mexican Family Favorites Cook Book*** by Maria Teresa Bermudez (144 pages)...***$5.00***

More than 200 recipes for Mexican festival desserts, custards, fruits, puddings, gelatines, cakes, pies, cookies, ice creams, sherbets and beverages. The only book of its kind! ***Mexican Desserts*** by Socorro Munoz Kimble and Irma Serrano Noriega (144 pages)...***$6.50***

INDEX

COYOLXAUHQUI

This circular stone, now on display in the Templo Mayor Museum, represents the defeat of Coyolxauhqui at the hands of her brother, Huitzilopochtli. She was the moon goddess and he was associated with the sun. (See pages 18 and 19 for a more detailed account.)